Psychopathology of Everyday Life

Sigmund Freud

Pharos Books

ISBN: 978-93-95229-38-8
eISBN: 978-93-95229-39-5

Publisher: Pharos Books (P) Ltd.
Plot No.-55, Main Mother Dairy Road
Pandav Nagar, East Delhi-110092
Phone: 011-40395855, +14049995474
WhatsApp: +91 8368220032
E-mail: sales@pharosbooks.in
Website: www.pharosbooks.in
First Edition: 2023

Printed By: Sushma Book Binding House, Okhla Industrial Area, Phase I, New Delhi-110020

Psychopathology of Everyday Life
Sigmund Freud

Contents

	INTRODUCTION	5
I.	FORGETTING OF PROPER NAMES	7
II.	FORGETTING OF FOREIGN WORDS	14
III.	FORGETTING OF NAMES AND ORDER OF WORDS	20
IV.	CHILDHOOD AND CONCEALING MEMORIES	36
V.	MISTAKES IN SPEECH	44
VI.	MISTAKES IN READING AND WRITING	70
VII.	FORGETTING OF IMPRESSIONS AND RESOLUTIONS	79
VIII.	ERRONEOUSLY CARRIED-OUT ACTIONS	100
IX.	SYMPTOMATIC AND CHANCE ACTIONS	121
X.	ERRORS	139
XI.	OMBINED FAULTY ACTS	147
XII.	DETERMINISM—CHANCE—AND SUPERSTITIOUS BELIEFS	153
	NOTES:	190

INTRODUCTION

Professor Freud developed his system of psychoanalysis while studying the so-called border-line cases of mental diseases, such as hysteria and compulsion neurosis. By discarding the old methods of treatment and strictly applying himself to a study of the patient's life he discovered that the hitherto puzzling symptoms had a definite meaning, and that there was nothing arbitrary in any morbid manifestation. Psychoanalysis always showed that they referred to some definite problem or conflict of the person concerned. It was while tracing back the abnormal to the normal state that Professor Freud found how faint the line of demarcation was between the normal and neurotic person, and that the psychopathologic mechanisms so glaringly observed in the psychoneuroses and psychoses could usually be demonstrated in a lesser degree in normal persons. This led to a study of the faulty actions of everyday life and later to the publication of the *Psychopathology of Everyday Life*, a book which passed through four editions in Germany and is considered the author's most popular work. With great ingenuity and penetration the author throws much light on the complex problems of human behaviour, and clearly demonstrates that the hitherto considered impassable gap between normal and abnormal mental states is more apparent than real.

This translation is made of the fourth German edition, and while the original text was strictly followed, linguistic difficulties often made it necessary to modify or substitute some of the author's cases by examples comprehensible to the English-speaking reader.

A. A. BRILL.
NEW YORK.

I

FORGETTING OF PROPER NAMES

During the year 1898 I published a short essay *On the Psychic Mechanism of Forgetfulness.*[1] I shall now repeat its contents and take it as a starting-point for further discussion. I have there undertaken a psychologic analysis of a common case of temporary forgetfulness of proper names, and from a pregnant example of my own observation I have reached the conclusion that this frequent and practically unimportant occurrence of a failure of a psychic function—of memory—admits an explanation which goes beyond the customary utilization of this phenomenon.

If an average psychologist should be asked to explain how it happens that we often fail to recall a name which we are sure we know, he would probably content himself with the answer that proper names are more apt to be forgotten than any other content of memory. He might give plausible reasons for this "forgetting preference" for proper names, but he would not assume any deep determinant for the process.

I was led to examine exhaustively the phenomenon of temporary forgetfulness through the observation of certain peculiarities, which, although not general, can, nevertheless, be seen clearly in some cases. In these there is not only *forgetfulness*, but also false *recollection*: he who strives for the escaped name brings to consciousness others—substitutive names—which, although immediately recognized as false, nevertheless obtrude themselves with great tenacity. The process which should lead to the reproduction of the lost name is, as it were, displaced, and thus brings one to an incorrect substitute.

Now it is my assumption that the displacement is not left to psychic arbitrariness, but that it follows lawful and rational paths. In other words, I assume that the substitutive name (or names) stands in direct relation to the lost name, and I hope, if I succeed in demonstrating this connection, to throw light on the origin of the forgetting of names.

In the example which I selected for analysis in 1898 I vainly strove to recall the name of the master who made the imposing frescoes of the "Last Judgment" in the dome of *Orvieto*. Instead of the lost name—*Signorelli*—two other names of artists—*Botticelli* and *Boltraffio*—obtruded themselves, names which my judgment immediately and definitely rejected as being incorrect. When the correct name was imparted to me by an outsider I recognized it at once without any hesitation. The examination of the influence and association paths which caused the displacement from *Signorelli* to *Botticelli* and *Boltraffio* led to the following results:—

(*a*) The reason for the escape of the name *Signorelli* is neither to be sought in the strangeness in itself of this name nor in the psychologic character of the connection in which it was inserted. The forgotten name was just as familiar to me as one of the substitutive names—Botticelli—and somewhat more familiar than the other substitute—Boltraffio—of the possessor of which I could hardly say more than that he belonged to the Milanese School. The connection, too, in which the forgetting of the name took place appeared to me harmless, and led to no further explanation. I journeyed by carriage with a stranger from Ragusa, Dalmatia, to a station in Herzegovina. Our conversation drifted to travelling in Italy, and I asked my companion whether he had been in Orvieto and had seen there the famous frescoes of——

(*b*) The forgetting of the name could not be explained until after I had recalled the theme discussed immediately before this conversation. This forgetting then made itself known *as a disturbance of the newly emerging theme caused by the theme preceding it.* In brief, before I asked my travelling companion if he had been in Orvieto we had been discussing the customs of the Turks living in *Bosnia* and *Herzegovina.* I had related what I heard from a colleague who was practising medicine among them, namely, that they show full confidence in the physician and complete submission to fate. When one is compelled to inform them that there is no help for the patient, they answer: "*Sir* (Herr), what can I say? I know that if he could be saved you would save him." In these sentences alone we can find the words and names: *Bosnia*, *Herzegovina*, and *Herr* (sir), which may be inserted in an association series between *Signorelli*, *Botticelli*, and *Boltraffio*.

(*c*) I assume that the stream of thoughts concerning the customs of the Turks in Bosnia, etc., was able to disturb the next thought, because I withdrew my attention from it before it came to an end. For I recalled that I wished to relate a second anecdote which was next to the first in my memory. These Turks value the sexual pleasure above all else, and at sexual disturbances merge into an utter despair which strangely contrasts with their resignation at the peril of losing their lives. One of my colleague's patients once told him: "For you know, sir (Herr), if that ceases, life no longer has any charm."

I refrained from imparting this characteristic feature because I did not wish to touch upon such a delicate theme in conversation with a stranger. But I went still further; I also deflected my attention from the continuation of the thought which might have associated itself in me with the theme "Death and Sexuality." I was at that time under the after-effects of a message which I had received a few weeks before, during a brief sojourn in *Trafoi*. A patient on whom I had spent much effort had ended his life on account of an incurable sexual disturbance. I know positively that this sad event, and everything connected with it, did not come to my conscious recollection on that trip in Herzegovina. However, the agreement between *Trafoi* and *Boltraffio* forces me to assume that this reminiscence was at that time brought to activity despite all the intentional deviation of my attention.

(*d*) I can no longer conceive the forgetting of the name Signorelli as an accidental occurrence. I must recognize in this process the influence of a *motive*. There were motives which actuated the interruption in the communication of my thoughts (concerning the customs of the Turks, etc.), and which later influenced me to exclude from my consciousness the thought connected with them, and which might have led to the message concerning the incident in Trafoi—that is, I wanted to forget something, I *repressed* something. To be sure, I wished to forget something other than the name of the master of Orvieto; but this other thought brought about an associative connection between itself and this name, so that my act of volition missed the aim, and I *forgot the one against my will*, while I *intentionally* wished to forget the other. The disinclination to recall directed itself against the one content; the inability to remember appeared in another. The case would have been obviously simpler if this disinclination and the inability to remember had concerned the same content. The substitutive names no longer seem so thoroughly justified as they were before this explanation. They remind me (after the form of a compromise) as much of what I wished to forget as of what I wished to remember, and show me that my object to forget something was neither a perfect success nor a failure.

(*e*) The nature of the association formed between the lost name and the repressed theme (death and sexuality, etc.), containing the names of Bosnia, Herzegovina, and Trafoi, is also very strange. In the scheme inserted here, which originally appeared in 1898, an attempt is made to graphically represent these associations.

The name Signorelli was thus divided into two parts. One pair of syllables (*elli*) returned unchanged in one of the substitutions, while the other had gained, through the translation of *signor* (sir, Herr), many and diverse relations to the name contained in the repressed theme, but was lost through it in the reproduction. Its substitution was formed in a way to suggest that a displacement took place along the same associations—"Herzegovina and Bosnia"—regardless of the sense and acoustic demarcation. The names were therefore treated in this process like the written pictures of a sentence which is to be transformed into a picture-puzzle (rebus). No information was given to consciousness concerning the whole process, which, instead of the name Signorelli, was thus changed to the substitutive names. At first sight no relation is apparent between the theme that contained the name Signorelli and the repressed one which immediately preceded it.

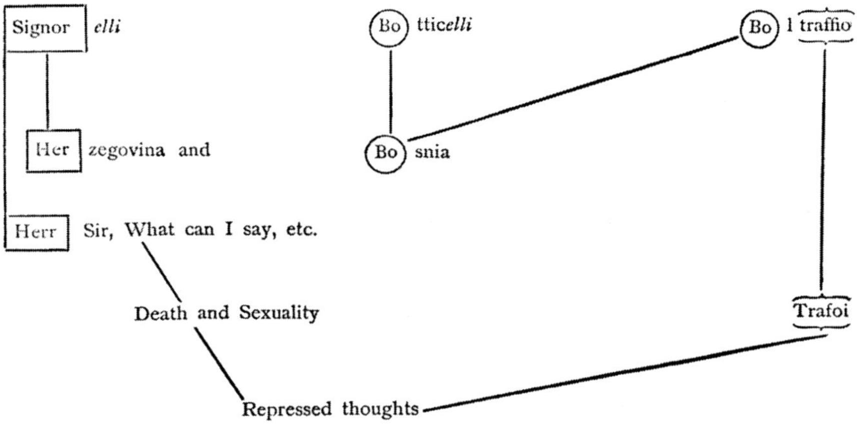

Perhaps it is not superfluous to remark that the given explanation does not contradict the conditions of memory reproduction and forgetting assumed by other psychologists, which they seek in certain relations and dispositions. Only in certain cases have we added another *motive* to the factors long recognized as causative in forgetting names, and have thus laid bare the mechanism of faulty memory. The assumed dispositions are indispensable also in our case, in order to make it possible for the repressed element to associatively gain control over the desired name and take it along into the repression. Perhaps this would not have occurred in another name having more favourable conditions of reproduction. For it is quite probable that a suppressed element continually strives to assert itself in some other way, but attains this success only where it meets with suitable conditions. At other times the suppression succeeds without disturbance of function, or, as we may justly say, without symptoms.

When we recapitulate the conditions for forgetting a name with faulty recollection we find:

(1) a certain disposition to forget the same;

(2) a process of suppression which has taken place shortly before; and

(3) the possibility of establishing an *outer* association between the concerned name and the element previously suppressed. The last condition will probably not have to be much overrated, for the slightest claim on the association is apt in most cases to bring it about. But it is a different and farther-reaching question whether such outer association can really furnish the proper condition to enable the suppressed element to disturb the reproduction of the desired name, or whether after all a more intimate connection between the two themes is not necessarily required. On superficial consideration one may be willing to reject the latter requirement and consider the temporal meeting in perfectly dissimilar contents as sufficient. But on more thorough examination one finds more and more frequently that the two elements (the repressed and the new one) connected by an outer association, possess besides a connection in content, and this can also be demonstrated in the example *Signorelli*.

The value of the understanding gained through the analysis of the example *Signorelli* naturally depends on whether we must explain this case as a typical or as an isolated process. I must now maintain that the forgetting of a name associated with faulty recollection uncommonly often follows the same process as was demonstrated in the case of *Signorelli*. Almost every time that I observed this phenomenon in myself I was able to explain it in the manner indicated above as being motivated by repression.

I must mention still another view-point in favour of the typical nature of our analysis. I believe that one is not justified in separating the cases of name-forgetting with faulty recollection from those in which incorrect substitutive names have not obtruded themselves. These substitutive names occur spontaneously in a number of cases; in other cases, where they do not come spontaneously, they can be brought to the surface by concentration of attention, and they then show the same relation to the repressed element and the lost name as those that come spontaneously. Two factors seem to play a part in bringing to consciousness the substitutive names: first, the effort of attention, and second, an inner determinant which adheres to the psychic material. I could find the latter in the greater or lesser facility which forms the required outer associations between the two elements. A great many of the cases of name-forgetting without faulty recollection therefore belong to the cases with substitutive name formation, the mechanism of which corresponds to the one in the example *Signorelli*. But I surely shall not venture to assert that all cases of name-forgetting belong to the same group. There is no doubt that there are cases of name-forgetting that proceed in a much simpler way. We shall represent this state of affairs carefully enough if we assert that *besides the simple forgetting of proper names there is another forgetting which is motivated by repression.*

***

II

FORGETTING OF FOREIGN WORDS

The ordinary vocabulary of our own language seems to be protected against forgetting within the limits of normal function, but it is quite different with words from a foreign language. The tendency to forget such words extends to all parts of speech. In fact, depending on our own general state and the degree of fatigue, the first manifestation of functional disturbance evinces itself in the irregularity of our control over foreign vocabulary. In a series of cases this forgetting follows the same mechanism as the one revealed in the example *Signorelli.* As a demonstration of this I shall report a single analysis, characterized, however, by valuable features, concerning the forgetting of a word, not a noun, from a Latin quotation. Before proceeding, allow me to give a full and clear account of this little episode.

Last summer, while journeying on my vacation, I renewed the acquaintance of a young man of academic education, who, as I soon noticed, was conversant with some of my works. In our conversation we drifted—I no longer remember how—to the social position of the race to which we both belonged. He, being ambitious, bemoaned the fact that his generation, as he expressed it, was destined to grow crippled, that it was prevented from developing its talents and from gratifying its desires. He concluded his passionately felt speech with the familiar verse from Virgil: *Exoriare* ... in which the unhappy *Dido* leaves her vengeance upon *Æneas* to posterity. Instead of "concluded," I should have said "wished to conclude," for he could not bring the quotation to an end, and attempted to conceal the open gap in his memory by transposing the words:—

"Exoriar(e) ex nostris ossibus ultor!"

He finally became piqued and said: "Please don't make such a mocking face, as if you were gloating over my embarrassment, but help me. There is something missing in this verse. How does it read in its complete form?"

"With pleasure," I answered, and cited it correctly:—

"Exoriar(e) aliquis nostris ex ossibus ultor!"

"It is too stupid to forget such a word," he said. "By the way, I understand you claim that forgetting is not without its reasons; I should be very curious to find out how I came to forget this indefinite pronoun '*aliquis*.'"

I gladly accepted the challenge, as I hoped to get an addition to my collection, and said, "We can easily do this, but I must ask you to tell me frankly and without any criticism everything that occurs to your mind after you focus your attention, without any particular intention, on the forgotten word."[2]

"Very well, the ridiculous idea comes to me to divide the word in the following way: *a* and *liquis*."

"What does that mean?"

"I don't know."

"What else does that recall to you?"

"The thought goes on to *reliques—liquidation—liquidity—fluid*."

"Does that mean anything to you now?"

"No, not by a long shot."

"Just go ahead."

"I now think," he said, laughing sarcastically, "of Simon of Trent, whose relics I saw two years ago in a church in Trent. I think of the old accusation which has been brought against the Jews again, and of the work of *Kleinpaul*, who sees in these supposed sacrifices reincarnations or revivals, so to speak, of the Saviour."

"This stream of thoughts has some connection with the theme which we discussed before the Latin word escaped you."

"You are right. I now think of an article in an Italian journal which I have recently read. I believe it was entitled: 'What St. Augustine said Concerning Women.' What can you do with this?"

I waited.

"Now I think of something which surely has no connection with the theme."

"Oh, please abstain from all criticism, and——"

"Oh, I know! I recall a handsome old gentleman whom I met on my journey last week. He was really an *original* type. He looked like a big bird of prey. His name, if you care to know, is Benedict."

"Well, at least you give a grouping of saints and Church fathers: *St. Simon*, *St. Augustine*, and *St. Benedict*. I believe that there was a Church father named *Origines*. Three of these, moreover, are Christian names, like *Paul* in the name *Kleinpaul*."

"Now I think of *St. Januarius* and his blood miracle—I find that the thoughts are running mechanically."

"Just stop a moment; both *St. Januarius* and *St. Augustine* have something to do with the calendar. Will you recall to me the blood miracle?"

"Don't you know about it? The blood of St. Januarius is preserved in a phial in a church in Naples, and on a certain holiday a miracle takes place causing it to liquefy. The people think a great deal of this miracle, and become very excited if the liquefying process is retarded, as happened once during the French occupation. The General in command—or Garibaldi, if I am not mistaken—then took the priest aside, and with a very significant gesture pointed out to him the soldiers arrayed without, and expressed his hope that the miracle would soon take place. And it actually took place...."

"Well, what else comes to your mind? Why do you hesitate?"

"Something really occurred to me ... but it is too intimate a matter to impart ... besides, I see no connection and no necessity for telling it."

"I will take care of the connection. Of course I cannot compel you to reveal what is disagreeable to you, but then you should not have demanded that I tell you why you forgot the word '*aliquis*.'"

"Really? Do you think so? Well, I suddenly thought of a woman from whom I could easily get a message that would be very annoying to us both."

"That she missed her courses?"

"How could you guess such a thing?"

"That was not very difficult. You prepared me for it long enough. Just think of the *saints of the calendar, the liquefying of the blood on a certain day, the excitement if the event does not take place, and the distinct threat that the miracle must take place....* Indeed, you have elaborated the miracle of St. Januarius into a clever allusion to the courses of the woman."

"It was surely without my knowledge. And do you really believe that my inability to reproduce the word '*aliquis*' was due to this anxious expectation?"

"That appears to me absolutely certain. Don't you recall dividing it into *a-liquis* and the associations: *reliques, liquidation, fluid*? Shall I also add to this connection the fact that St. Simon, to whom you got by way of the *reliques*, was sacrificed as a child?"

"Please stop. I hope you do not take these thoughts—if I really entertained them—seriously. I will, however, confess to you that the lady is Italian, and that I visited Naples in her company. But may not all this be coincidental?"

"I must leave to your own judgment whether you can explain all these connections through the assumption of coincidence. I will tell you, however, that every similar case that you analyse will lead you to just such remarkable 'coincidences!'"

I have more than one reason for valuing this little analysis, for which I am indebted to my travelling companion. First, because in this case I was able to make use of a source which is otherwise inaccessible to me. Most of the examples of psychic disturbances of daily life that I have here compiled I was obliged to take from observation of myself. I endeavoured to evade the far richer material furnished me by my neurotic patients, because I had to preclude the objection that the phenomena in question were only the result and manifestation of the neurosis. It was therefore of special value for my purpose to have a stranger free from a neurosis offer himself as a subject for such examination. This analysis is also important in other respects, inasmuch as it elucidates a case of word-forgetting *without* substitutive recollection, and thus confirms the principle formulated above, namely, that the appearance or nonappearance of incorrect substitutive recollections does not constitute an essential distinction[3].

But the principal value of the example *aliquis* lies in another of its distinctions from the case *Signorelli*. In the latter example the reproduction of the name becomes disturbed through the after-effects of a stream of thought which began shortly before and was interrupted, but whose content had no distinct relation to the new theme which contained the name Signorelli. Between the repression and the theme of the forgotten name there existed only the relation of temporal contiguity, which reached the other in order that the two should be able to form a connection through an outer association.[4] On the other hand, in the example *aliquis* one can note no trace of such an independent repressed theme which could occupy conscious thought immediately before and then re-echo as a disturbance. The disturbance of the reproduction proceeded here from the inner part of the theme touched upon, and was brought about by the fact that unconsciously a contradiction arose against the wish-idea represented in the quotation.

The origin must be construed in the following manner: The speaker deplored the fact that the present generation of his people was being deprived of its rights, and like Dido he presaged that a new generation would take upon itself vengeance against the oppressors. He therefore expressed the wish for posterity. In this moment he was interrupted by the contradictory thought: "Do you really wish so much for posterity? That is not true. Just think in what a predicament you would be if you should now receive the information that you must expect posterity from the quarter you have in mind! No, you want no posterity—as much as you need it for your vengeance." This contradiction asserts itself, just as in the example *Signorelli*, by forming an outer association between one of his ideation elements and an element of the repressed wish, but here it is brought about in a most strained manner through what seems an artificial detour of associations. Another important agreement with the example *Signorelli* results from the fact that the contradiction originates from repressed sources and emanates from thoughts which would cause a deviation of attention.

So much for the diversity and the inner relationship of both paradigms of the forgetting of names. We have learned to know a second mechanism of forgetting, namely, the disturbance of thought through an inner contradiction emanating from the repression. In the course of this discussion we shall repeatedly meet with this process, which seems to me to be the more easily understood.

***

III

FORGETTING OF NAMES AND ORDER OF WORDS

Experiences like those mentioned concerning the process of forgetting a part of the order of words from a foreign language may cause one to wonder whether the forgetting of the order of words in one's own language requires an essentially different explanation. To be sure, one is not wont to be surprised if after awhile a formula or poem learned by heart can only be reproduced imperfectly, with variations and gaps. Still, as this forgetting does not affect equally all the things learned together, but seems to pick out therefrom definite parts, it may be worth our effort to investigate analytically some examples of such faulty reproductions.

Brill reports the following example:—

"While conversing one day with a very brilliant young woman she had occasion to quote from Keats. The poem was entitled 'Ode to Apollo,' and she recited the following lines:—

> "'In thy western house of gold
> Where thou livest in thy state,
> Bards, that once sublimely told
> Prosaic truths that came too late.'

She hesitated many times during the recitation, being sure that there was something wrong with the last line. To her great surprise, on referring to the book she found that not only was the last line misquoted but that there were many other mistakes. The correct lines read as follows:—

ODE TO APOLLO

"'In thy western *halls* of gold
When thou *sittest* in thy state,
Bards, that *erst* sublimely told
Heroic deeds and sang of fate.'

The words italicized are those that have been forgotten and replaced by others during the recitation.

"She was astonished at her many mistakes, and attributed them to a failure of memory. I could readily convince her, however, that there was no qualitative or quantitative disturbance of memory in her case, and recalled to her our conversation immediately before quoting these lines.

"We were discussing the over-estimation of personality among lovers, and she thought it was Victor Hugo who said that love is the greatest thing in the world because it makes an angel or a god out of a grocery clerk. She continued: 'Only when we are in love have we blind faith in humanity; everything is perfect, everything is beautiful, and ... everything is so poetically unreal. Still, it is a wonderful experience; worth going through, notwithstanding the terrible disappointments that usually follow. It puts us on a level with the gods and incites us to all sorts of artistic activities. We become real poets; we not only memorize and quote poetry, but we often become Apollos ourselves.' She then quoted the lines given above.

"When I asked on what occasion she memorized the lines she could not recall. As a teacher of elocution she was wont to memorize so much and so often that it was difficult to tell just when she had memorized these lines. 'Judging by the conversation,' I suggested, 'it would seem that this poem is intimately associated with the idea of over-estimation of personality of one in love. Have you perhaps memorized this poem when you were in such a state?' She became thoughtful for a while and soon recalled the following facts: Twelve years before, when she was eighteen years old, she fell in love. She met the young man while participating in an amateur theatrical performance. He was at the time studying for the stage, and it was predicted that some day he would be a matinée idol. He was endowed with all the attributes needed for such a calling. He was well built, fascinating, impulsive, very clever, and ... very fickle-minded. She was warned against him, but she paid no heed, attributing it all to the envy of her counsellors. Everything went well for a few months, when she suddenly received word that her Apollo, for whom she had memorized these lines, had eloped with and married a very wealthy young woman. A few years later she heard that he was living in a Western city, where he was taking care of his father-in-law's interests.

"The misquoted lines are now quite plain. The discussion about the over-estimation of personality among lovers unconsciously recalled to her a disagreeable experience, when she herself over-estimated the personality of the man she loved. She thought he was a god, but he turned out to be even worse than the average mortal. The episode could not come to the surface because it was determined by very disagreeable and painful thoughts, but the unconscious variations in the poem plainly showed her present mental state. The poetic expressions were not only changed to prosaic ones, but they clearly alluded to the whole episode."

Another example of forgetting the order of words of a poem well known to the person I shall cite from Dr. C. G. Jung,[5] quoting the words of the author:—

"A man wished to recite the familiar poem, 'A Pine-tree Stands Alone,' etc. In the line 'He felt drowsy' he became hopelessly stuck at the words 'with the white sheet.' This forgetting of such a well-known verse seemed to me rather peculiar, and I therefore asked him to reproduce what came to his mind when he thought of the words 'with the white sheet.' He gave the following series of associations 'The white sheet makes one think of a white sheet on a corpse—a linen sheet with which one covers a dead body—pause. —now I think of a near friend—his brother died quite recently—he is supposed to have died of heart disease—he was also very corpulent—my friend is corpulent, too, and I thought that he might meet the same fate—

probably he doesn't exercise enough—when I heard of this death I suddenly became frightened: the same thing might happen to me, as my own family is predisposed to obesity—my grandfather died of heart disease—I, also, am somewhat too corpulent, and for that reason I began an obesity cure a few days ago.'"

Jung remarks: "The man had unconsciously immediately identified himself with the pine-tree which was covered with a white sheet."

For the following example of forgetting the order of words I am indebted to my friend Dr. Ferenczi, of Budapest. Unlike the former examples, it does not refer to a verse taken from poetry, but to a self-coined saying. It may also demonstrate to us the rather unusual case where the forgetting places itself at the disposal of discretion when the latter is in danger of yielding to a momentary desire. The mistake thus advances to a useful function. After we have sobered down we justify that inner striving which at first could manifest itself only by way of inability, as in forgetting or psychic impotence.

"At a social gathering some one quoted, *Tout comprendre c'est tout pardonner*, to which I remarked that the first part of the sentence should suffice, as 'pardoning' is an exemption which must be left to God and the priest. One of the guests thought this observation very good, which in turn emboldened me to remark—probably to ensure myself of the good opinion of the well-disposed critic—that some time ago I thought of something still better. But when I was about to repeat this clever idea I was unable to recall it. Thereupon I immediately withdrew from the company and wrote my concealing thoughts. I first recalled the name of the friend who had witnessed the birth of this (desired) thought, and of the street in Budapest where it took place, and then the name of another friend, whose name was Max, whom we usually called Maxie. That led me to the word 'maxim,' and to the thought that at that time, as in the present case, it was a question of varying a well-known maxim. Strangely enough, I did not recall any maxim but the following sentence: '*God created man in His own image*,' and its changed conception, '*Man created God in his own image*.' Immediately I recalled the sought-for recollection.

"My friend said to me at that time in Andrassy Street, '*Nothing human is foreign to me.*' To which I remarked, basing it on psychoanalytic experience, 'You should go further and acknowledge *that nothing animal is foreign to you.*'

"But after I had finally found the desired recollection I was even then prevented from telling it in this social gathering. The young wife of the friend whom I had reminded of the animality of the unconscious was also among those present, and I was perforce reminded that she was not at all prepared for the reception of such unsympathetic views. The forgetting spared me a number of unpleasant questions from her and a hopeless discussion, and just that must have been the motive of the 'temporary amnesia.'

"It is interesting to note that as a concealing thought there emerged a sentence in which the deity is degraded to a human invention, while in the sought-for sentence there was an allusion to the animal in the man. The *capitis diminutio* is therefore common to both. The whole matter was apparently only a continuation of the stream of thought concerning understanding and forgiving which was stimulated by the discussion.

"That the desired thought so rapidly appeared may be also due to the fact that I withdrew into a vacant room, away from the society in which it was censored."

I have since then analysed a large number of cases of forgetting or faulty reproduction of the order of words, and the consistent result of these investigations led me to assume that the mechanisms of forgetting, as demonstrated in the examples "*aliquis*" and "*Ode to Apollo*," are almost of universal validity. It is not always very convenient to report such analyses, for, just as those cited, they usually lead to intimate and painful things in the person analysed; I shall therefore add no more to the number of such examples. What is common to all these cases, regardless of the material, is the fact that the forgotten or distorted material becomes connected through some associative road with an unconscious stream of thought, which gives rise to the influence that comes to light as forgetting.

I am now returning to the forgetting of names, concerning which we have so far considered exhaustively neither the casuistic elements nor the motives. As this form of faulty acts can at times be abundantly observed in myself, I am not at a loss for examples. The slight attacks of migraine, from which I am still suffering, are wont to announce themselves hours before through the forgetting of names, and at the height of the attack, during which I am not forced, however, to give up my work, I am often unable to recall all proper names.

Still, just such cases as mine may furnish the cause for a strong objection to our analytic efforts. Should not one be forced to conclude from such observations that the causation of the forgetfulness, especially the forgetting of names, is to be sought in circulatory or functional disturbances of the brain, and spare himself the trouble of searching for psychologic explanations for these phenomena? Not at all; that would mean to interchange the mechanism of a process, which is the same in all cases, with its variations. But instead of an analysis I shall cite a comparison which will settle the argument.

Let us assume that I was so reckless as to take a walk at night in an uninhabited neighbourhood of a big city, and was attacked and robbed of my watch and purse. At the nearest police-station I report the matter in the following words: "I was in this or that street, and was there robbed of my watch and purse by *lonesomeness* and *darkness*." Although these words would not express anything that is incorrect, I would, nevertheless, run the danger of being considered—judging from the wording of this report—as not quite right in the head. To be correct, the state of affairs could only be described by saying that, *favoured* by the lonesomeness of the place and under *cover* of darkness, I was robbed of my valuables by *unknown malefactors.*

Now, then, the state of affairs in forgetting names need not be different. Favoured by exhaustion, circulatory disturbances, and intoxication, I am robbed by an unknown psychic force of the disposal over the proper names belonging to my memory; it is the same force which in other cases may bring about the same failure of memory during perfect health and mental capacity.

When I analyse those cases of name-forgetting occurring in myself, I find almost regularly that the name withheld shows some relation to a theme which concerns my own person, and is apt to provoke in me strong and often painful emotions. Following the convenient and commendable practice of the Zurich School (Bleuler, Jung, Riklin), I might express the same thing in the following form: The name withheld has touched a "personal complex" in me. The relation of the name to my person is an unexpected one, and is mostly brought about through superficial associations (words of double meaning and of similar sounds); it may generally be designated as a side association. A few simple examples will best illustrate the nature of the same:—

(*a*) A patient requested me to recommend to him a sanatorium in the Riviera. I knew of such a place very near Genoa, I also recalled the name of the German colleague who was in charge of the place, but the place itself I could not name, well as I believed I knew it. There was nothing left to do but ask the patient to wait, and to appeal quickly to the women of the family. "Just what is the name of the place near Genoa where Dr. X. has his small institution in which Mrs. So-and-so remained so long under treatment?" "Of course you would forget a name of that sort. The name is Nervi." To be sure, I have enough to do with nerves.

(*b*) Another patient spoke about a neighbouring summer resort, and maintained that besides the two familiar inns there was a third. I disputed the existence of any third inn, and referred to the fact that I had spent seven summers in the vicinity and therefore knew more about the place than he. Instigated by my contradiction, he recalled the name. The name of the third inn was "The Hochwartner." Of course, I had to admit it; indeed, I was forced to confess that for seven summers I had lived near this very inn whose existence I had so strenuously denied. But why should I have forgotten the name and the object? I believe because the name sounded very much like that of a Vienna colleague who practised the same specialty as my own. It touched in me the "professional complex."

(*c*) On another occasion, when about to buy a railroad ticket on the Reichenhall Station, I could not recall the very familiar name of the next big railroad station which I had so often passed. I was forced to look it up in the time-table. The name was Rosehome (Rosenheim). I soon discovered through what associations I lost it. An hour earlier I had visited my sister in her home near Reichenhall; my sister's name is Rose, hence also a Rosehome. This name was taken away by my "family complex."

(*d*) This predatory influence of the "family complex" I can demonstrate in a whole series of complexes. One day I was consulted by a young man, a younger brother of one of my female patients, whom I saw any number of times, and whom I used to call by his first name. Later, while wishing to talk about his visit, I forgot his first name, in no way an unusual one, and could not recall it in any way. I walked into the street to read the business signs and recognized the name as soon as it met my eyes. The analysis showed that I had formed a parallel between the visitor and my own brother which centred in the question: "Would my brother, in a similar case, have behaved like him or even more contrarily?" The outer connection between the thoughts concerning the stranger and my own family was rendered possible through the accident that the name of the mothers in each case was the same, Amelia. Subsequently I also understood the substitutive names, Daniel and Frank, which obtruded themselves without any explanation. These names, as well as Amelia, belong to Schiller's play *The Robbers*; they are all connected with a joke of the Vienna pedestrian, Daniel Spitzer.

(*e*) On another occasion I was unable to find a patient's name which had a certain reference to my early life. The analysis had to be followed over a long devious road before the desired name was discovered. The patient expressed his apprehension lest he should lose his eyesight; this recalled a young man who became blind from a gunshot, and this again led to a picture of another youth who shot himself, and the latter bore the same name as my first patient, though not at all related to him. The name became known to me, however, only after the anxious apprehension from these two juvenile cases was transferred to a person of my own family. Thus an incessant stream of "self-reference" flows through my thoughts concerning which I usually have no inkling, but which betrays itself through such name-forgetting. It seems as if I were forced to compare with my own person all that I hear about strangers, as if my personal complexes became stirred up at every information from others. It seems impossible that this should be an individual peculiarity of my own person; it must, on the contrary, point to the way we grasp outside matters in general. I have reasons to assume that other individuals meet with experiences quite similar to mine. The best example of this kind was reported to me by a gentleman named Lederer as a personal experience. While on his wedding trip in Venice he came across a man with whom he was but slightly acquainted, and whom he was obliged to introduce to his wife. As he forgot the name of the stranger he got himself out of the embarrassment the first time by mumbling the name unintelligibly. But when he met the man a second time, as is inevitable in Venice, he took him aside and begged him to help him out of the difficulty by telling him his name, which he unfortunately had forgotten. The answer of the stranger pointed to a superior knowledge of human nature: "I readily believe that you did not grasp my name. My name is like yours—Lederer!" One cannot suppress a slight feeling of unpleasantness on discovering his own name in a stranger. I had recently felt it very plainly when I was consulted during my office hours by a man named S. Freud. However, I am assured by one of my own critics that in this respect he behaves in quite the opposite manner.

(*f*) The effect of personal relation can be recognized also in the following examples reported by Jung.[6] "Mr. Y. falls in love with a lady who soon thereafter marries Mr. X. In spite of the fact that Mr. Y. was an old acquaintance of Mr. X., and had business relations with him, he repeatedly forgot the name, and on a number of occasions, when wishing to correspond with X., he was obliged to ask other people for his name." However, the motivation for the forgetting is more evident in this case than in the preceding ones, which were under the constellation of the personal reference. Here the forgetting is manifestly a direct result of the dislike of Y. for the happy rival; he does not wish to know anything about him.

(*g*) The following case, reported by Ferenczi, the analysis of which is especially instructive through the explanation of the substitutive thoughts (like *Botticelli-Boltraffio* to *Signorelli*), shows in a somewhat different way how self-reference leads to the forgetting of a name:—"A lady who heard something about psychoanalysis could not recall the name of the psychiatrist, Young (Jung). "Instead, the following names occurred to her: Kl. (a name)—Wilde—Nietzsche—Hauptmann. "I did not tell her the name, and requested her to repeat her free associations to every thought. "To Kl. she at once thought of Mrs. Kl., that she was an embellished and affected person who looked very well for her age. 'She does not age.' As a general and principal conception of Wilde and Nietzsche, she gave the association 'mental disease.' She then added jocosely: 'The Freudians will continue looking for the causes of mental diseases until they themselves become insane.' She continued: 'I cannot bear Wilde and Nietzsche. I do not understand them. I hear that they were both homosexual. Wilde has occupied himself with *young* people' (although she uttered in this sentence the correct name she still could not remember it). "To Hauptmann she associated the words *half* and *youth*, and only after I called her attention to the word *youth* did she become aware that she was looking for the name Young (Jung)." It is clear that this lady, who had lost her husband at the age of thirty-nine, and had no prospect of marrying a second time, had cause enough to avoid reminiscences recalling youth or old age. The remarkable thing is that the concealing thoughts of the desired name came to the surface as simple associations of content without any sound-associations.

(*h*) Still different and very finely motivated is an example of name-forgetting which the person concerned has himself explained. "While taking an examination in philosophy as a minor subject I was questioned by the examiner about the teachings of Epicurus, and was asked whether I knew who took up his teachings centuries later. I answered that it was Pierre Gassendi, whom two days before while in a café I had happened to hear spoken of as a follower of Epicurus. To the question how I knew this I boldly replied that I had taken an interest in Gassendi for a long time. This resulted in a certificate with a *magna cum laude*, but later, unfortunately, also in a persistent tendency to forget the name Gassendi. I believe that it is due to my guilty conscience that even now I cannot retain this name despite all efforts. I had no business knowing it at that time."

To have a proper appreciation of the intense repugnance entertained by our narrator against the recollection of this examination episode, one must have realized how highly he prizes his doctor's degree, and for how many other things this substitute must stand.

I add here another example of forgetting the name of a city, an instance which is perhaps not as simple as those given before, but which will appear credible and valuable to those more familiar with such investigations. The name of an Italian city withdrew itself from memory on account of its far-reaching sound-similarity to a woman's first name, which was in turn connected with various emotional reminiscences which were surely not exhaustively treated in this report. Dr. S. Ferenczi, who observed this case of forgetting in himself, treated it—quite justly—as an analysis of a dream or an erotic idea.

"To-day I visited some old friends, and the conversation turned to cities of Northern Italy. Some one remarked that they still showed the Austrian influence. A few of these cities were cited. I, too, wished to mention one, but the name did not come to me, although I knew that I had spent two very pleasant days there; this, of course, does not quite concur with Freud's theory of forgetting. Instead of the desired name of the city there obtruded themselves the following thoughts: 'Capua—Brescia—the lion of Brescia.' This lion I saw objectively before me in the form of a marble statue, but I soon noticed that he resembled less the lion of the statue of liberty in Brescia (which I saw only in a picture) than the other marble lion which I saw in

Lucerne on the monument in honour of the Swiss Guard fallen in the Tuileries. I finally thought of the desired name: it was Verona. "I knew at once the cause of this amnesia. No other than a former servant of the family whom I visited at the time. Her name was Veronica; in Hungarian Verona. I felt a great antipathy for her on account of her repulsive physiognomy, as well as her hoarse, shrill voice and her unbearable self-assertion (to which she thought herself entitled on account of her long service). Also the tyrannical way in which she treated the children of the family was insufferable to me. Now I knew the significance of the substitutive thoughts. "To Capua I immediately associated *caput mortuum*. I had often compared Veronica's head to a skull. The Hungarian word *kapzoi* (greed after money) surely furnished a determinant for the displacement. Naturally I also found those more direct associations which connected Capua and Verona as geographical ideas and as Italian words of the same rhythm. "The same held true for Brescia; here, too, I found concealed side-tracks of associations of ideas. "My antipathy at that time was so violent that I thought Veronica very ugly, and have often expressed my astonishment at the fact that any one should love her: 'Why, to kiss her,' I said, 'must provoke nausea.' "Brescia, at least in Hungary, is very often mentioned not in connection with the lion but with another wild beast. The most hated name in this country, as well as in North Italy, is that of General Haynau, who is briefly referred to as the hyena of Brescia. From the hated tyrant Haynau one stream of thought leads over Brescia to the city of Verona, and the other over the idea of the *grave-digging animal with the hoarse voice* (which corresponds to the thought of a monument to the dead), to the skull, and to the disagreeable organ of Veronica, which was so cruelly insulted in my unconscious mind. Veronica in her time ruled as tyrannically as did the Austrian General after the Hungarian and Italian struggles for liberty. "Lucerne is associated with the idea of the summer which Veronica spent with her employers in a place near Lucerne. The Swiss Guard again recalls that she tyrannized not only the children but also the adult members of the family, and thus played the part of the 'Garde-Dame.'

"I expressly observe that this antipathy of mine against V. consciously belongs to things long overcome. Since that time she has changed in her appearance and manner, very much to her advantage, so that I am able to meet her with sincere regard (to be sure I hardly find such occasion). As usual, however, my unconscious sticks more tenaciously to those impressions; it is old in its resentment. "The Tuileries represent an allusion to a second personality, an old French lady who actually 'guarded' the women of the house, and who was in high regard and somewhat feared by everybody. For a long time I was her *élève* in French conversation. The word *élève* recalls that when I visited the brother-in-law of my present host in northern Bohemia I had to laugh a great deal because the rural population referred to the *élèves* (pupils) of the school of forestry as *löwen* (lions). Also this jocose recollection might have taken part in the displacement of the hyena by the lion."

(*i*) The following example can also show how a personal complex swaying the person at the time being may by devious ways bring about the forgetting of a name.[7] Two men, an elder and a younger, who had travelled together in Sicily six months before, exchanged reminiscences of those pleasant and interesting days.

"Let's see, what was the name of that place," asked the younger, "where we passed the night before taking the trip to Selinunt? *Calatafini*, was it not?"

The elder rejected this by saying: "Certainly not; but I have forgotten the name, too, although I can recall perfectly all the details of the place. Whenever I hear some one forget a name it immediately produces forgetfulness in me. Let us look for the name. I cannot think of any other name except *Caltanisetta*, which is surely not correct."

"No," said the younger, "the name begins with, or contains, a *w*."

"But the Italian language contains no *w*," retorted the elder.

"I really meant a *v*, and I said *w* because I am accustomed to interchange them in my mother tongue."

The elder, however, objected to the *v*. He added: "I believe that I have already forgotten many of the Sicilian names. Suppose we try to find out. For example, what is the name of the place situated on a height which was called *Enna* in antiquity?"

"Oh, I know that: *Castrogiovanni*." In the next moment the younger man discovered the lost name. He cried out '*Castelvetrano*,' and was pleased to be able to demonstrate the supposed *v*.

For a moment the elder still lacked the feeling of recognition, but after he accepted the name he was able to state why it had escaped him. He thought: "Obviously because the second half, *vetrano*, suggests *veteran*. I am aware that I am not quite anxious to think of ageing, and react peculiarly when I am reminded of it. Thus, *e.g.*, I had recently reminded a very esteemed friend in most unmistakable terms that he had 'long ago passed the years of youth,' because before this he once remarked in the most flattering manner, 'I am no longer a young man.' That my resistance was directed against the second half of the name *Castelvetrano* is shown by the fact that the initial sound of the same returned in the substitutive name Caltanisetta."

"What about the name Caltanisetta itself?" asked the younger.

"That always seemed to me like a pet name of a young woman," admitted the elder.

Somewhat later he added: "The name for *Enna* was also only a substitutive name. And now it occurs to me that the name *Castrogiovanni*, which obtruded itself with the aid of a rationalization, alludes as expressly to *giovane*, young, as the last name, *Castelvetrano*, to *veteran*."

The older man believed that he had thus accounted for his forgetting the name. What the motive was that led the young man to this memory failure was not investigated.

In some cases one must have recourse to all the fineness of psychoanalytic technique in order to explain the forgetting of a name. Those who wish to read an example of such work I refer to a communication by Professor E. Jones.[8]

I could multiply the examples of name-forgetting and prolong the discussion very much further if I did not wish to avoid elucidating here almost all the view-points which will be considered in later themes. I shall, however, take the liberty of comprehending in a few sentences the results of the analyses reported here.

The mechanism of forgetting, or rather of losing or temporary forgetting of a name, consists in the disturbance of the intended reproduction of the name through a strange stream of thought unconscious at the time. Between the disturbed name and the disturbing complex there exists a connection either from the beginning or such a connection has been formed—perhaps by artificial means—through superficial (outer) associations.

The self-reference complex (personal, family or professional) proves to be the most effective of the disturbing complexes.

A name which by virtue of its many meanings belongs to a number of thought associations (complexes) is frequently disturbed in its connection to one series of thoughts through a stronger complex belonging to the other associations.

To avoid the awakening of pain through memory is one of the objects among the motives of these disturbances.

In general one may distinguish two principal cases of name-forgetting; when the name itself touches something unpleasant, or when it is brought into connection with other associations which are influenced by such effects. So that names can be disturbed on their own account or on account of their nearer or more remote associative relations in the reproduction.

A review of these general principles readily convinces us that the temporary forgetting of a name is observed as the most frequent faulty action of our mental functions.

However, we are far from having described all the peculiarities of this phenomenon. I also wish to call attention to the fact that name-forgetting is extremely contagious. In a conversation between two persons the mere mention of having forgotten this or that name by one often suffices to induce the same memory slip in the other. But wherever the forgetting is induced, the sought for name easily comes to the surface.

There is also a continuous forgetting of names in which whole chains of names are withdrawn from memory. If in the course of endeavouring to discover an escaped name one finds others with which the latter is intimately connected, it often happens that these new names also escape. The forgetting thus jumps from one name to another, as if to demonstrate the existence of a hindrance not to be easily removed.

***

IV

CHILDHOOD AND CONCEALING MEMORIES

In a second essay[9] I was able to demonstrate the purposive nature of our memories in an unexpected field. I started with the remarkable fact that the earliest recollections of a person often seemed to preserve the unimportant and accidental, whereas (frequently though not universally!) not a trace is found in the adult memory of the weighty and affective impressions of this period. As it is known that the memory exercises a certain selection among the impressions at its disposal, it would seem logical to suppose that this selection follows entirely different principles in childhood than at the time of intellectual maturity. However, close investigation points to the fact that such an assumption is superfluous. The indifferent childhood memories owe their existence to a process of displacement. It may be shown by psychoanalysis that in the reproduction they represent the substitute for other really significant impressions, whose direct reproduction is hindered by some resistance. As they do not owe their existence to their own contents, but to an associative relation of their contents to another repressed thought, they deserve the title of "concealing memories," by which I have designated them.

In the aforementioned essay I only touched upon, but in no way exhausted, the varieties in the relations and meanings of concealed memories. In the given example fully analysed I particularly emphasized a peculiarity in the temporal relation between the concealing memory and the contents of the memory concealed by it. The content of the concealing memory in that example belonged to one of the first years of childhood, while the thoughts represented by it, which remained practically unconscious, belonged to a later period of the individual in question. I called this form of displacement a retro-active or *regressive* one. Perhaps more often one finds the reversed relation—that is, an indifferent impression of the most remote period becomes a concealing memory in consciousness, which simply owes its existence to an association with an earlier experience, against whose direct reproduction there are resistances. We would call these *encroaching* or *interposing* concealing memories. What most concerns the memory lies here chronologically beyond the concealing memory. Finally, there may be a third possible case, namely, the concealing memory may be connected with the impression it conceals, not only through its contents, but also through contiguity of time; this is the *contemporaneous* or *contiguous* concealing memory.

How large a portion of the sum total of our memory belongs to the category of concealing memories, and what part it plays in various neurotic hidden processes, these are problems into the value of which I have neither inquired nor shall I enter here. I am concerned only with emphasizing the sameness between the forgetting of proper names with faulty recollection and the formation of concealing memories.

At first sight it would seem that the diversities of both phenomena are far more striking than their exact analogies. There we deal with proper names, here with complete impressions experienced either in reality or in thought; there we deal with a manifest failure of the memory function, here with a memory act which appears strange to us. Again, there we are concerned with a momentary disturbance—for the name just forgotten could have been reproduced correctly a hundred times before, and will be so again from to-morrow on; here we deal with lasting possession without a failure, for the indifferent childhood memories seem to be able to accompany us through a great part of life. In both these cases the riddle seems to be solved in an entirely different way. There it is the forgetting, while here it is the remembering which excites our scientific curiosity.

After deeper reflection one realizes that, although there is a diversity in the psychic material and in the duration of time of the two phenomena, yet these are by far outweighed by the conformities between the two. In both cases we deal with the failure of remembering: what should be correctly reproduced by the memory fails to appear, and instead something else comes as a substitute. In the case of forgetting a name there is no lack of memory function in the form of name substitution. The formation of a concealing memory depends on the forgetting of other important impressions. In both cases we are reminded by an intellectual feeling of the intervention of a disturbance, which in each case takes a different form. In the case of forgetting of names we are aware that the substitutive names are incorrect, while in concealing memories we are surprised that we have them at all. Hence, if psychologic analysis demonstrates that the substitutive formation in each case is brought about in the same manner—that is, through displacement along a superficial association—we are justified in saying that the diversities in material, in duration of time, and in the centring of both phenomena serve to enhance our expectation, that we have discovered something that is important and of general value. This generality purports that the stopping and straying of the reproducing function indicates more often than we suppose that there is an intervention of a prejudicial factor, a tendency which favours one memory and at the same time works against another.

The subject of childhood memories appears to me so important and interesting that I would like to devote to it a few additional remarks which go beyond the views expressed so far.

How far back into childhood do our memories reach? I am familiar with some investigations on this question by V. and C. Henri[10] and Potwin.[11] They assert that such examinations show wide individual variations, inasmuch as some trace their first reminiscences to the sixth month of life, while others can recall nothing of their lives before the end of the sixth or even the eighth year. But what connection is there between these variations in the behaviour of childhood reminiscences, and what signification may be ascribed to them? It seems that it is not enough to procure the material for this question by simple inquiry, but it must later be subjected to a study in which the person furnishing the information must participate.

I believe we accept too indifferently the fact of infantile amnesia—that is, the failure of memory for the first years of our lives—and fail to find in it a strange riddle. We forget of what great intellectual accomplishments and of what complicated emotions a child of four years is capable. We really ought to wonder why the memory of later years has, as a rule, retained so little of these psychic processes, especially as we have every reason for assuming that these same forgotten childhood activities have not glided off without leaving a trace in the development of the person, but that they have left a definite influence for all future time. Yet in spite of this unparalleled effectiveness they were forgotten! This would suggest that there are particularly formed conditions of memory (in the sense of conscious reproduction) which have thus far eluded our knowledge. It is quite possible that the forgetting of childhood may give us the key to the understanding of those amnesias which, according to our newer studies, lie at the basis of the formation of all neurotic symptoms.

Of these retained childhood reminiscences, some appear to us readily comprehensible, while others seem strange or unintelligible. It is not difficult to correct certain errors in regard to both kinds. If the retained reminiscences of a person are subjected to an analytic test, it can be readily ascertained that a guarantee for their correctness does not exist. Some of the memory pictures are surely falsified and incomplete, or displaced in point of time and place. The assertions of persons examined that their first memories reach back perhaps to their second year are evidently unreliable. Motives can soon be discovered which explain the disfigurement and the displacement of these experiences, but they also demonstrate that these memory lapses are not the result of a mere unreliable memory. Powerful forces from a later period have moulded the memory capacity of our infantile experiences, and it is probably due to these same forces that the understanding of our childhood is generally so very strange to us.

The recollection of adults, as is known, proceeds through different psychic material. Some recall by means of visual pictures—their memories are of a visual character; other individuals can scarcely reproduce in memory the most paltry sketch of an experience; we call such persons "*auditifs*" and "*moteurs*" in contrast to the "*visuels*," terms proposed by Charcot. These differences vanish in dreams; all our dreams are preponderatingly visual. But this development is also found in the childhood memories; the latter are plastic and visual, even in those people whose later memory lacks the visual element. The visual memory, therefore, preserves the type of the infantile recollections. Only my earliest childhood memories are of a visual character; they represent plastically depicted scenes, comparable only to stage settings.

In these scenes of childhood, whether they prove true or false, one usually sees his own childish person both in contour and dress. This circumstance must excite our wonder, for adults do not see their own persons in their recollections of later experiences.[12] It is, moreover, against our experiences to assume that the child's attention during his experiences is centred on himself rather than exclusively on outside impressions. Various sources force us to assume that the so-called earliest childhood recollections are not true memory traces but later elaborations of the same, elaborations which might have been subjected to the influences of many later psychic forces. Thus the "childhood reminiscences" of individuals altogether advance to the signification of "concealing memories," and thereby form a noteworthy analogy to the childhood reminiscences as laid down in the legends and myths of nations.

Whoever has examined mentally a number of persons by the method of psychoanalysis must have gathered in this work numerous examples of concealing memories of every description. However, owing to the previously discussed nature of the relations of the childhood reminiscences to later life, it becomes extraordinarily difficult to report such examples. For, in order to attach the value of the concealing memory to an infantile reminiscence, it would be often necessary to present the entire life-history of the person concerned. Only seldom is it possible, as in the following good example, to take out from its context and report a single childhood memory.

A twenty-four-year-old man preserved the following picture from the fifth year of his life: In the garden of a summer-house he sat on a stool next to his aunt, who was engaged in teaching him the alphabet. He found difficulty in distinguishing the letter *m* from *n*, and he begged his aunt to tell him how to tell one from the other. His aunt called his attention to the fact that the letter *m* had one whole portion (a stroke) more than the letter *n*. There was no reason to dispute the reliability of this childhood recollection; its meaning, however, was discovered only later, when it showed itself to be the symbolic representation of another boyish inquisitiveness. For just as he wanted to know the difference between *m* and *n* at that time, so he concerned himself later about the difference between boy and girl, and he would have been willing that just this aunt should be his teacher. He also discovered that the difference was a similar one; that the boy again had one whole portion more than the girl, and at the time of this recognition his memory awoke to the corresponding childish inquisitiveness.

I would like to show by one more example the sense that may be gained by a childhood reminiscence through analytic work, although it may seem to contain no sense before. In my forty-third year, when I began to interest myself in what remained in my memory of my own childhood, a scene struck me which for a long time, as I afterwards believed, had repeatedly come to consciousness, and which through reliable identification could be traced to a period before the completion of my third year. I saw myself in front of a chest, the door of which was held open by my half-brother, twenty years my senior. I stood there demanding something and screaming; my mother, pretty and slender, then suddenly entered the room, as if returning from the street.

In these words I formulated this scene so vividly seen, which, however, furnished no other clue. Whether my brother wished to open or lock the chest (in the first explanation it was a "cupboard"), why I cried, and what bearing the arrival of my mother had, all these questions were dim to me; I was tempted to explain to myself that it dealt with the memory of a hoax by my older brother, which was interrupted by my mother. Such misunderstandings of childhood scenes retained in memory are not uncommon; we recall a situation, but it is not centralized; we do not know on which of the elements to place the psychic accent. Analytic effort led me to an entirely unexpected solution of the picture. I missed my mother and began to suspect that she was locked in this cupboard or chest, and therefore demanded that my brother should unlock it. As he obliged me, and I became convinced that she was not in the chest, I began to cry; this is the moment firmly retained in the memory, which was directly followed by the appearance of my mother, who appeased my worry and anxiety.

But how did the child get the idea of looking for the absent mother in the chest? Dreams which occurred at the same time pointed dimly to a nurse, concerning whom other reminiscences were retained; as, for example, that she conscientiously urged me to deliver to her the small coins which I received as gifts, a detail which in itself may lay claim to the value of a concealing memory for later things. I then concluded to facilitate for myself this time the task of interpretation, and asked my now aged mother about that nurse. I found out all sorts of things, among others the fact that this shrewd but dishonest person had committed extensive robberies during the confinement of my mother, and that my half-brother was instrumental in bringing her to justice.

This information gave me the key to the scene from childhood, as through a sort of inspiration. The sudden disappearance of the nurse was not a matter of indifference to me; I had just asked this brother where she was, probably because I had noticed that he had played a part in her disappearance, and he, evasive and witty as he is to this day, answered that she was "boxed in." I understood this answer in the childish way, but asked no more, as there was nothing else to be discovered. When my mother left me shortly thereafter I suspected that the naughty brother had treated her in the same way as he did the nurse, and therefore pressed him to open the chest.

I also understand now why in the translation of the visual childhood scene my mother's slenderness was accentuated; she must have struck me as being newly restored. I am two and a half years older than the sister born at that time, and when I was three years of age I was separated from my half-brother.

***

V

MISTAKES IN SPEECH

Although the ordinary material of speech of our mother-tongue seems to be guarded against forgetting, its application, however, more often succumbs to another disturbance which is familiar to us as "slips of the tongue." What we observe in normal persons as slips of the tongue gives the same impression as the first step of the so-called "paraphasias" which manifest themselves under pathologic conditions.

I am in the exceptional position of being about to refer to a previous work on the subject. In the year 1895 Meringer and C. Mayer published a study on *Mistakes in Speech and Reading*, with whose view-points I do not agree. One of the authors, who is the spokesman in the text, is a philologist actuated by a linguistic interest to examine the rules governing those slips. He hoped to deduce from these rules the existence "of a definite psychic mechanism," "whereby the sounds of a word, of a sentence, and even the words themselves, would be associated and connected with one another in a quite peculiar manner" (p. 10).

The authors grouped the examples of speech-mistakes collected by them first according to purely descriptive view-points, such as interchangings (*e.g.*, the Milo of Venus instead of the Venus of Milo), as anticipations (*e.g.*, the shoes made her sorft ... the shoes made her feet sore), as echoes and post positions, as contaminations (*e.g.*, "I will soon him home," instead of "I will soon go home and I will see him"), and substitutions (*e.g.*, "he entrusted his money to a savings crank," instead of "a savings bank").[13] Besides these principal categories there are some others of lesser importance (or of lesser significance for our purpose). In this grouping it makes no difference whether the transposition, disfigurement, fusion, etc., affects single sounds of the word or syllables, or whole words of the concerned sentence.

To explain the various forms of mistakes in speech, Meringer assumes a varied psychic value of phonetics. As soon as the innervation affects the first syllable of a word, or the first word of a sentence, the stimulating process immediately strikes the succeeding sounds, and the following words, and in so far as these innervations are synchronous they may effect some changes in one another. The stimulus of the psychically more intensive sound "rings" before or continues echoing, and thus disturbs the less important process of innervation. It is necessary therefore to determine which are the most important sounds of a word. Meringer states: "If one wishes to know which sound of a word possesses the greatest intensity he should examine himself while searching for a forgotten word, for example, a name. That which first returns to consciousness invariably had the greatest intensity prior to the forgetting (p. 160). Thus the most important sounds are the initial sound of the root-syllable and the initial sound of the word itself, as well as one or another of the accentuated vowels" (p. 162).

Here I cannot help voicing a contradiction. Whether or not the initial sound of the name belongs to the most important elements of the word, it is surely not true that in the case of the forgetting of the word it first returns to consciousness; the above rule is therefore of no use. When we observe ourselves during the search for a forgotten name we are comparatively often forced to express the opinion that it begins with a certain letter. This conviction proves to be as often unfounded as founded. Indeed, I would even go so far as to assert that in the majority of cases one reproduces a false initial sound. Also in our example *Signorelli* the substitutive name lacked the initial sound, and the principal syllables were lost; on the other hand, the less important pair of syllables *elli* returned to consciousness in the substitutive name *Botticelli*.

How little substitutive names respect the initial sound of the lost names may be learned from the following case. One day I found it impossible to recall the name of the small country whose capital is Monte Carlo. The substitutive names were as follows: *Piedmont*, *Albania*,

Montevideo, *Colico*. In place of Albania *Montenegro* soon appeared, and then it struck me that the syllable *Mont* (pronounced *Mon*) occurred in all but the last of the substitutive names. It thus became easy for me to find from the name of Prince Albert the forgotten name *Monaco*. *Colico* practically imitates the syllabic sequence and rhythm of the forgotten name.

If we admit the conjecture that a mechanism similar to that pointed out in the forgetting of names may also play a part in the phenomena of speech-blunders, we are then led to a better founded judgment of cases of speech-blunders. The speech disturbance which manifests itself as a speech-blunder may in the first place be caused by the influence of another component of the same speech, that is, through a fore-sound or an echo, or through another meaning within the sentence or context which differs from that which the speaker wishes to utter. In the second place, however, the disturbance could be brought about analogously to the process in the case *Signorelli*, through influences outside this word, sentence or context, from elements which we did not intend to express, and of whose incitement we became conscious only through the disturbance. In both modes of origin of the mistake in speech the common element lies in the simultaneity of the stimulus, while the differentiating elements lie in the arrangement within or without the same sentence or context.

The difference does not at first appear as wide as when it is taken into consideration in certain conclusions drawn from the symptomatology of speech-mistakes. It is clear, however, that only in the first case is there a prospect of drawing conclusions from the manifestations of speech-blunders concerning a mechanism which connects together sounds and words for the reciprocal influence of their articulation; that is, conclusions such as the philologist hopes to gain from the study of speech-blunders. In the case of disturbance through influence outside of the same sentence or context, it would before all be a question of becoming acquainted with the disturbing elements, and then the question would arise whether the mechanism of this disturbance cannot also suggest the probable laws of the formation of speech.

We cannot maintain that Meringer and Mayer have overlooked the possibility of speech disturbance through "complicated psychic influences," that is, through elements outside of the same word or sentence or the same sequence of words. Indeed, they must have observed that the theory of the psychic variation of sounds applies, strictly speaking, only to the explanation of sound disturbances as well as to fore-sounds and after-sounds. Where the word disturbances cannot be reduced to sound disturbances, as, for example, in the substitutions and contaminations of words, they, too, have without hesitation sought the cause of the mistake in speech outside of the intended context, and proved this state of affairs by means of fitting examples.[14] According to the author's own understanding it is some similarity between a certain word in the intended sentence and some other not intended, which allows the latter to assert itself in consciousness by causing a disfigurement, a composition, or a compromise formation (contamination).

Now, in my work on the *Interpretation of Dreams* I have shown the part played by the process of condensation in the origin of the so-called manifest contents of the dream from the latent thoughts of the dream. Any similarity of objects or of word-presentations between two elements of the unconscious material is taken as a cause for the formation of a third, which is a composite or compromise formation. This element represents both components in the dream content, and in view of this origin it is frequently endowed with numerous contradictory individual determinants. The formation of substitutions and contaminations in speech-mistakes is, therefore, the beginning of that work of condensation which we find taking a most active part in the construction of the dream.

In a small essay destined for the general reader,[15] Meringer advanced a theory of very practical significance for certain cases of interchanging of words, especially for such cases where one word is substituted by another of opposite meaning. He says: "We may still recall the manner in which the President of the Austrian House of Deputies opened the session some time ago: 'Honoured Sirs! I announce the presence of so and so many gentlemen, and therefore declare the session as "closed"'!" The general merriment first attracted his attention and he corrected his mistake. In the present case the probable explanation is that the President wished himself in a position to close this session, from which he had little good to expect, and the thought broke through at least partially—a frequent manifestation—resulting in his use of "closed" in place of "opened," that is, the opposite of the statement intended. Numerous observations have taught me, however, that we frequently interchange contrasting words; they are already associated in our speech consciousness; they lie very close together and are easily incorrectly evoked.

Still, not in all cases of contrast substitution is it so simple as in the example of the President as to appear plausible that the speech-mistake occurs merely as a contradiction which arises in the inner thought of the speaker opposing the sentence uttered. We have found the analogous mechanism in the analysis of the example *aliquis*; there the inner contradiction asserts itself in the form of forgetting a word instead of a substitution through its opposite. But in order to adjust the difference we may remark that the little word *aliquis* is incapable of a contrast similar to "closing" and "opening," and that the word "opening" cannot be subject to forgetting on account of its being a common component of speech.

Having been shown by the last examples of Meringer and Mayer that speech disturbance may be caused through the influence of fore-sounds, after-sounds, words from the same sentence that were intended for expression, as well as through the effect of words outside the sentence intended, *the stimulus of which would otherwise not have been suspected*, we shall next wish to discover whether we can definitely separate the two classes of mistakes in speech, and how we can distinguish the example of the one from a case of the other class.

But at this stage of the discussion we must also think of the assertions of Wundt, who deals with the manifestations of speech-mistakes in his recent work on the development of language.[16] Psychic influences, according to Wundt, never lack in these as well as in other phenomena related to them. "The uninhibited stream of *sound* and *word associations* stimulated by spoken sounds belongs here in the first place as a positive determinant. This is supported as a negative factor by the relaxation or suppression of the influences of the will which inhibit this stream, and by the active attention which is here a function of volition. Whether that play of association manifests itself in the fact that a coming sound is anticipated or a preceding sound reproduced, or whether a familiar practised sound becomes intercalated between others, or finally, whether it manifests itself in the fact that altogether different sounds associatively related to the spoken sounds act upon these—all these questions designate only differences in the direction, and at most in the play of the occurring associations but not in the general nature of the same. In some cases it may be also doubtful to which form a certain disturbance may be attributed, or whether it would not be more correct to refer such disturbance to a concurrence of many motives, *following the principle of the complication of causes*[17] (cf. pp. 380-81)."

I consider these observations of Wundt as absolutely justified and very instructive. Perhaps we could emphasize with even greater firmness than Wundt that the positive factor favouring mistakes in speech (the uninhibited stream of associations, and its negative, the relaxation of the inhibiting attention) regularly attain synchronous action, so that both factors become only different determinants of the same process. With the relaxation, or, more unequivocally expressed, *through* this relaxation, of the inhibiting attention the uninhibited stream of associations becomes active.

Among the examples of the mistakes in speech collected by me I can scarcely find one in which I would be obliged to attribute the speech disturbance simply and solely to what Wundt calls "contact effect of sound." Almost invariably I discover besides this a disturbing influence of something outside of the intended speech. The disturbing element is either a single unconscious thought, which comes to light through the speech-blunder, and can only be brought to consciousness through a searching analysis, or it is a more general psychic motive, which directs itself against the entire speech.

(*Example a*) Seeing my daughter make an unpleasant face while biting into an apple, I wished to quote the following couplet:—

"The ape he is a funny sight,
When in the apple he takes a bite."

But I began: "The apel...." This seems to be a contamination of "ape" and "apple" (compromise formation), or it may be also conceived as an anticipation of the prepared "apple." The true state of affairs, however, was this: I began the quotation once before, and made no mistake the first time. I made the mistake only during the repetition, which was necessary because my daughter, having been distracted from another side, did not listen to me. This repetition with the added impatience to disburden myself of the sentence I must include in the motivation of the speech-blunder, which represented itself as a function of condensation.

(*b*) My daughter said, "I wrote to Mrs. Schresinger." The woman's name was Schlesinger. This speech-blunder may depend on the tendency to facilitate articulation. I must state, however, that this mistake was made by my daughter a few moments after I had said *apel* instead of *ape*. Mistakes in speech are in a great measure contagious; a similar peculiarity was noticed by Meringer and Mayer in the forgetting of names. I know of no reason for this psychic contagiousness.

(*c*) "I *sut* up like a pocket-knife," said a patient in the beginning of treatment, instead of "I *shut* up." This suggests a difficulty of articulation which may serve as an excuse for the interchanging of sounds. When her attention was called to the speech-blunder, she promptly replied, "Yes, that happened because you said '*earnesht*' instead of '*earnest*.'" As a matter of fact I received her with the remark, "To-day we shall be in earnest" (because it was the last hour before her discharge from treatment), and I jokingly changed the word into *earnesht*. In the course of the hour she repeatedly made mistakes in speech, and I finally observed that it was not only because she imitated me but because she had a special reason in her unconscious to linger at the word earnest (Ernst) as a name.[18]

(*d*) A woman, speaking about a game invented by her children and called by them "the man in the box," said "the manx in the boc." I could readily understand her mistake. It was while analysing her dream, in which her husband is depicted as very generous in money matters—just the reverse of reality—that she made this speech-blunder. The day before she had asked for a new set of furs, which her husband denied her, claiming that he could not afford to spend so much money. She upbraided him for his stinginess, "for putting away so much into the strong-box," and mentioned a friend whose husband has not nearly his income, and yet he presented his wife with a *mink* coat for her birthday. The mistake is now comprehensible. The word *manx* (*manks*) reduces itself to the "minks" which she longs for, and the *box* refers to her husband's stinginess.

(*e*) A similar mechanism is shown in the mistake of another patient whose memory deserted her in the midst of a long-forgotten childish reminiscence. Her memory failed to inform her on what part of the body the prying and lustful hand of another had touched her. Soon thereafter she visited one of her friends, with whom she discussed summer homes. Asked where her cottage in M. was located, she answered, "Near the *mountain loin*" instead of "*mountain lane*."

(*f*) Another patient, whom I asked at the end of her visit how her uncle was, answered: "I don't know, I only see him now *in flagranti*." The following day she said, "I am really ashamed of myself for having given you yesterday such a stupid answer. Naturally you must have thought me a very uneducated person who always mistakes the meaning of foreign words. I wished to say *en passant*." We did not know at the time where she got the incorrectly used foreign words, but during the same session she reproduced a reminiscence as a continuation of the theme from the previous day, in which being caught *in flagranti* played the principal part. The mistake of the previous day had therefore anticipated the recollection, which at that time had not yet become conscious.

(*g*) In discussing her summer plans, a patient said, "I shall remain most of the summer in *Elberlon*." She noted her mistake, and asked me to analyse it. The associations to *Elberlon* elicited: seashore on the Jersey coast—summer resort—vacation travelling. This recalled travelling in Europe with her cousin, a topic which we had discussed the day before during the analysis of a dream. The dream dealt with her dislike for this cousin, and she admitted that it was mainly due to the fact that the latter was the favourite of the man whom they met together while travelling abroad. During the dream analysis she could not recall the name of the city in which they met this man, and I did not make any effort at the time to bring it to her consciousness, as we were engrossed in a totally different problem. When asked to focus her attention again on Elberlon and reproduce her associations, she said, "It brings to mind *Elberlawn—lawn—field*—and *Elberfield*." *Elberfeld* was the lost name of the city in Germany. Here the mistake served to bring to consciousness in a concealed manner a memory which was connected with a painful feeling.

(*h*) A woman said to me, "If you wish to buy a carpet, go to *Merchant* (Kaufmann) in *Matthew Street* (Mathäusgasse)." I repeated, "Then at Matthew's—I mean at Merchant's——" It would seem that my repeating of one name in place of the other was simply the result of distraction. The woman's remark really did distract me, as she turned my attention to something else much more vital to me than carpet. In Matthew Street stands the house in which my wife lived as a bride. The entrance to the house was in another street, and now I noticed that I had forgotten its name and could only recall it through a roundabout method. The name Matthew, which kept my attention, is thus a substitutive name for the forgotten name of the street. It is more suitable than the name Merchant, for Matthew is exclusively the name of a person, while Merchant is not. The forgotten street, too, bears the name of a person: *Radetzky*.

(*i*) A patient consulted me for the first time, and from her history it became apparent that the cause of her nervousness was largely an unhappy married life. Without any encouragement she went into details about her marital troubles. She had not lived with her husband for about six months, and she saw him last at the theatre, when she saw the play *Officer 606*. I called her attention to the mistake, and she immediately corrected herself, saying that she meant to say *Officer 666* (the name of a recent popular play). I decided to find out the reason for the mistake, and as the patient came to me for analytic treatment, I discovered that the immediate cause of the rupture between herself and husband was the disease which is treated by "606."[19]

(*k*) Before calling on me a patient telephoned for an appointment, and also wished to be informed about my consultation fee. He was told that the first consultation was ten dollars; after the examination was over he again asked what he was to pay, and added: "I don't like to owe money to any one, especially to doctors; I prefer to pay right away." Instead of *pay* he said *play*. His last voluntary remarks and his mistake put me on my guard, but after a few more uncalled-for remarks he set me at ease by taking money from his pocket. He counted four paper dollars and was very chagrined and surprised because he had no more money with him, and promised to send me a cheque for the balance. I was sure that his mistake betrayed him, that he was only *playing* with me, but there was nothing to be done. At the end of a few weeks I sent him a bill for the balance, and the letter was returned to me by the post-office authorities marked "Not found."

(*l*) Miss X. spoke very warmly of Mr. Y., which was rather strange, as before this she had always expressed her indifference, not to say her contempt, for him. On being asked about this sudden change of heart she said: "I really never had anything against him; he was always nice to me, but I never gave him the chance to cultivate my acquaintance." She said "cuptivate." This neologism was a contamination of *cultivate* and *captivate*, and foretold the coming betrothal.

(*m*) An illustration of the mechanisms of contamination and condensation will be found in the following *lapsus linguæ*. Speaking of Miss Z., Miss W. depicted her as a very "straitlaced" person who was not given to levities, etc. Miss X. thereupon remarked: "Yes, that is a very characteristic description, she always appealed to me as very '*straicet-brazed*.'" Here the mistake resolved itself into *straitlaced* and *brazen-faced*, which corresponded to Miss W.'s opinion of Miss Z.

(*n*) I shall quote a number of examples from a paper by my colleague, Dr. W. Stekel, which appeared in the Berlin *Tageblatt* of January, 1904, entitled "Unconscious Confessions." "An unpleasant trick of my unpleasant thoughts was revealed by the following example: To begin with, I may state that in my capacity as a physician I never consider my remuneration, but always keep in view the patient's interest only: this goes without saying. I was visiting a patient who was convalescing from a serious illness. We had passed through hard days and nights. I was happy to find her improved, and I portrayed to her the pleasures of a sojourn in Abbazia, concluding with: 'If, as I hope, you will *not* soon leave your bed.' This obviously came from an unconscious selfish motive, to be able to continue treating this wealthy patient, a wish which is entirely foreign to my waking consciousness, and which I would reject with indignation."

(*o*) Another example (Dr. W. Stekel): "My wife engaged a French governess for the afternoons, and later, coming to a satisfactory agreement, wished to retain her testimonials. The governess begged to be allowed to keep them, saying, 'Je cherche encore pour les *après-midis*—pardons, pour les *avant-midis*.' She apparently intended to seek another place which would perhaps offer more profitable arrangements—an intention which she carried out."

(*p*) I was to give a lecture to a woman. Her husband, upon whose request this was done, stood behind the door listening. At the end of my sermonizing, which had made a visible impression, I said: "Good-bye, sir!" To the experienced person I thus betrayed the fact that the words were directed towards the husband; that I had spoken to oblige him.

(*q*) Dr. Stekel reports about himself that he had under treatment at the same time two patients from Triest, each of whom he always addressed incorrectly. "Good morning, Mr. Peloni!" he would say to Askoli, and to Peloni, "Good morning, Mr. Askoli!" He was at first inclined to attribute no deeper motive to this mistake, but to explain it through a number of similarities in both persons. However, he easily convinced himself that here the interchange of names bespoke a sort of boast—that is, he was acquainting each of his Italian patients with the fact that neither was the only resident of Triest who came to Vienna in search of his medical advice.

(*r*) Two women stopped in front of a drug-store, and one said to her companion, "If you will wait a few *moments* I'll soon be back," but she said *movements* instead. She was on her way to buy some castoria for her child.

(*s*) Mr. L., who is fonder of being called on than of calling, spoke to me through the telephone from a nearby summer resort. He wanted to know when I would pay him a visit. I reminded him that it was his turn to visit me, and called his attention to the fact that, as he was the happy possessor of an automobile, it would be easier for him to call on me. (We were at different summer resorts, separated by about one half-hour's railway trip.) He gladly promised to call, and asked: "How about Labour Day (September 1st), will it be convenient for you?" When I answered affirmatively, he said, "Very well, then, put me down for *Election* Day" (November). His mistake was quite plain. He likes to visit me, but it was inconvenient to travel so far. In November we would both be in the city. My analysis proved correct.

(*t*) A friend described to me a nervous patient, and wished to know whether I could benefit him. I remarked: "I believe that in time I can remove all his symptoms by psychoanalysis, because it is a durable case," wishing to say "curable"!

(*u*) I repeatedly addressed my patient as Mrs. Smith, her married daughter's name, when her real name is Mrs. James. My attention having been called to it, I soon discovered that I had another patient of the same name who refused to pay for the treatment. Mrs. Smith was also my patient and paid her bills promptly.

(*v*) A *lapsus linguæ* sometimes stands for a particular characteristic. A young woman, who is the domineering spirit in her home, said of her ailing husband that he had consulted the doctor about a wholesome diet for himself, and then added: "The doctor said that diet has nothing to do with his ailments, and that he can eat and drink what *I* want."

(*w*) I cannot omit this excellent and instructive example, although, according to my authority, it is about twenty years old. A lady once expressed herself in society—the very words show that they were uttered with fervour and under the pressure of a great many secret emotions: "Yes, a woman must be pretty if she is to please the men. A man is much better off. As long as he has *five* straight limbs, he needs no more!"

This example affords us a good insight into the intimate mechanisms of a mistake in speech by means of condensation and contamination (cf. p. 72). It is quite obvious that we have here a fusion of two similar modes of expression:—

"As long as he has his four *straight limbs*."
"As long as he has all his *five senses*."

Or the term "straight" may be the common element of the two intended expressions:—

"As long as he has his straight limbs."
"All five should be straight."

It may also be assumed that both modes of expression—viz., those of the five senses and those of the straight five—have co-operated to introduce into the sentence about the straight limbs first a number and then the mysterious five instead of the simple four. But this fusion surely would not have succeeded if it had not expressed good sense in the form resulting from the mistake; if it had not expressed a cynical truth which, naturally, could not be uttered unconcealed, coming as it did from a woman. Finally, we shall not hesitate to call attention to the fact that the woman's saying, following its wording, could just as well be an excellent witticism as a jocose speech-blunder. It is simply a question whether she uttered these words with conscious or unconscious intention. The behaviour of the speaker in this case certainly speaks against the conscious intention, and thus excludes wit.

(*x*) Owing to similarity of material, I add here another case of speech-blunder, the interpretation of which requires less skill. A professor of anatomy strove to explain the nostril, which, as is known, is a very difficult anatomical structure. To his question whether his audience grasped his ideas he received an affirmative reply. The professor, known for his self-esteem, thereupon remarked: "I can hardly believe this, for the number of people who understand the nostril, even in a city of millions like Vienna, can be counted *on a finger*—pardon me, I meant to say *on the fingers* of a hand."

(*y*) I am indebted to Dr. Alf. Robitsek, of Vienna, for calling my attention to two speech-blunders from an old French author, which I shall reproduce in the original.

Brantôme (1527-1614), *Vies des Dames galantes*, Discours second: "Si ay-je cogneu une très belle et honneste dame de par le monde, qui, devisant avec un honneste gentilhomme de la cour des affaires de la guerre durant ces civiles, elle luy dit: 'J'ay ouy dire que le roy a faiet rompre tous les c—— de ce pays là.' Elle vouloit dire le ponts. Pensez que, venant de coucher d'avec son mary, ou songeant à son amant, elle avoit encor ce nom frais en la bouche; et le gentilhomme s'en eschauffer en amours d'elle pour ce mot.

"Une autre dame que j'ai cogneue, entretenant une autre grand dame plus qu'elle, et luy louant et exaltant ses beautez, elle luy dit après: 'Non, madame, ce que je vous en dis, ce n'est point pour vous *adultérer*'; voulant dire *adulater*, comme elle le rhabilla ainsi: pensez qu'elle songeoit à adultérer."

In the psychotherapeutic procedure which I employ in the solution and removal of neurotic symptoms, I am often confronted with the task of discovering from the accidental utterances and fancies of the patient the thought contents, which, though striving for concealment, nevertheless unintentionally betray themselves. In doing this the mistakes often perform the most valuable service, as I can show through most convincing and still most singular examples.

For example, patients speak of an aunt and later, without noting the mistake, call her "my mother," or designate a husband as a "brother." In this way they attract my attention to the fact that they have "identified" these persons with each other, that they have placed them in the same category, which for their emotional life signifies the recurrence of the same type. Or, a young man of twenty years presents himself during my office hours with these words: "I am the father of N. N., whom you have treated—pardon me, I mean the brother; why, he is four years older than I." I understand through this mistake that he wishes to express that, like the brother, he, too, is ill through the fault of the father; like his brother, he wishes to be cured, but that the father is the one most in need of treatment. At other times an unusual arrangement of words, or a forced expression, is sufficient to disclose in the speech of the patient the participation of a repressed thought having a different motive.

Hence, in coarse as well as in finer speech disturbances, which may, nevertheless, be subsumed as "speech-blunders," I find that it is not the contact effects of the sound, but the thoughts outside the intended speech, which determine the origin of the speech-blunder, and also suffice to explain the newly formed mistakes in speech. I do not doubt the laws whereby the sounds produce changes upon one another; but they alone do not appear to me sufficiently forcible to mar the correct execution of speech. In those cases which I have studied and investigated more closely they merely represent the preformed mechanism, which is conveniently utilized by a more remote psychic motive. The latter does not, however, form a part of the sphere of influence of these sound relations. *In a large number of substitutions caused by mistakes in talking there is an entire absence of such phonetic laws.* In this respect I am in full accord with Wundt, who likewise assumes that the conditions underlying speech-blunders are complex and go far beyond the contact effect of the sounds.

If I accept as certain "these more remote psychic influences," following Wundt's expression, there is still nothing to detain me from conceding also that in accelerated speech, with a certain amount of diverted attention, the causes of speech-blunder may be easily limited to the definite law of Meringer and Mayer. However, in a number of examples gathered by these authors a more complicated solution is quite apparent.

In some forms of speech-blunders we may assume that the disturbing factor is the result of striking against obscene words and meanings. The purposive disfigurement and distortion of words and phrases, which is so popular with vulgar persons, aims at nothing else but the employing of a harmless motive as a reminder of the obscene, and this sport is so frequent that it would not be at all remarkable if it appeared unintentionally and contrary to the will.

I trust that the readers will not depreciate the value of these interpretations, for which there is no proof, and of these examples which I have myself collected and explained by means of analysis. But if secretly I still cherish the expectation that even the apparently simple cases of speech-blunder will be traced to a disturbance caused by a half-repressed idea outside of the intended context, I am tempted to it by a noteworthy observation of Meringer. This author asserts that it is remarkable that nobody wishes to admit having made a mistake in speaking. There are many intelligent and honest people who are offended if we tell them that they made a mistake in speaking. I would not risk making this assertion as general as does Meringer, using the term "nobody." But the emotional trace which clings to the demonstration of the mistake, which manifestly belongs to the nature of shame, has its significance. It may be classed with the anger displayed at the inability to recall a forgotten name, and with the surprise at the tenaciousness of an apparently indifferent memory, and it invariably points to the participation of a motive in the formation of the disturbance.

The distorting of names amounts to an insult when done intentionally, and could have the same significance in a whole series of cases where it appears as unintentional speech-blunders. The person who, according to Mayer's report, once said "Freuder" instead of "Freud," because shortly before he pronounced the name "Breuer" (p. 38), and who at another time spoke of the "Freuer-Breudian" method (p. 28), was certainly not particularly enthusiastic over this method.

Later, under the mistakes in writing, I shall report a case of name disfigurement which certainly admits of no other explanation.[20]

As a disturbing element in these cases there is an intermingling of a criticism which must be omitted, because at the time being it does not correspond to the intention of the speaker.

Or it may be just the reverse; the substituted name, or the adoption of the strange name, signifies an appreciation of the same. The identification which is brought about by the mistake is equivalent to a recognition which for the moment must remain in the background. An experience of this kind from his schooldays is related by Dr. Ferenczi:—

"While in my first year at college I was obliged to recite a poem before the whole class. It was the first experience of the kind in my life, but I was well prepared. As soon as I began my recitation I was dismayed at being disturbed by an outburst of laughter. The professor later explained to me this strange reception. I started by giving the title 'From the Distance,' which was correct, but instead of giving the name of the real author, I mentioned—my own. The name of the poet is Alexander Petöfi. The identity of the first name with my own favoured the interchange of names, but the real reason was surely the fact that I identified myself at that time with the celebrated poet-hero. Even consciously I entertained for him a love and respect which verged on adoration. The whole ambition-complex hides itself under this faulty action."

A similar identification was reported to me concerning a young physician who timidly and reverently introduced himself to the celebrated Virchow with the following words: "I am Dr. Virchow." The surprised professor turned to him and asked, "Is your name also Virchow?" I do not know how the ambitious young man justified his speech-blunder, whether he thought of the charming excuse that he imagined himself so insignificant next to this big man that his own name slipped from him, or whether he had the courage to admit that he hoped that he, too, would some day be as great a man as Virchow, and that the professor should therefore not treat him in too disparaging a manner. One or both of these thoughts may have put this young man in an embarrassing position during the introduction.

Owing to very personal motives I must leave it undecided whether a similar interpretation may also apply in the case to be cited. At the International Congress in Amsterdam, in 1907, my theories of hysteria were the subject of a lively discussion. One of my most violent opponents, in his diatribe against me, repeatedly made mistakes in speech in such a manner that he put himself in my place and spoke in my name. He said, for example, "Breuer and I, as is well known, have demonstrated," etc., when he wished to say "Breuer and Freud." The name of this opponent does not show the slightest sound similarity to my own. From this example, as well as from other cases of interchanging names in speech-blunders, we are reminded of the fact that the speech-blunder can fully forego the facility afforded to it through similar sounds, and can achieve its purpose if only supported in content by concealed relations.

In other and more significant cases it is a self-criticism, an internal contradiction against one's own utterance, which causes the speech-blunder, and even forces a contrasting substitution for the one intended. We then observe with surprise how the wording of an assertion removes the purpose of the same, and how the error in speech lays bare the inner dishonesty. Here the *lapsus linguæ* becomes a mimicking form of expression, often, indeed, for the expression of what one does not wish to say. It is thus a means of self-betrayal.

Brill relates: "I had recently been consulted by a woman who showed many paranoid trends, and as she had no relatives who could co-operate with me, I urged her to enter a State hospital as a voluntary patient. She was quite willing to do so, but on the following day she told me that her friends with whom she leased an apartment objected to her going to a hospital, as it would interfere with their plans, and so on. I lost patience and said: 'There is no use listening to your friends who know nothing about your mental condition; you are quite *incompetent* to take care of your own affairs.' I meant to say 'competent.' Here the *lapsus linguæ* expressed my true opinion."

Favoured by chance the speech material often gives origin to examples of speech-blunders which serve to bring about an overwhelming revelation or a full comic effect, as shown by the following examples reported by Brill:—

"A wealthy but not very generous host invited his friends for an evening dance. Everything went well until about 11.30 p.m., when there was an intermission, presumably for supper. To the great disappointment of most of the guests there was no supper; instead, they were regaled with thin sandwiches and lemonade. As it was close to Election day the conversation centred on the different candidates; and as the discussion grew warmer, one of the guests, an ardent admirer of the Progressive Party candidate, remarked to the host: 'You may say what you please about Teddy, but there is one thing—he can always be relied upon; he always gives you a *square meal*,' wishing to say *square deal*. The assembled guests burst into a roar of laughter, to the great embarrassment of the speaker and the host, who fully understood each other."

"While writing a prescription for a woman who was especially weighed down by the financial burden of the treatment, I was interested to hear her say suddenly: 'Please do not give me *big bills*, because I cannot swallow them.' Of course she meant to say *pills*."

The following example illustrates a rather serious case of self-betrayal through a mistake in talking. Some accessory details justify full reproduction as first printed by Dr. A. A. Brill.[21]

"While walking one night with Dr. Frink we accidentally met a colleague, Dr. P., whom I had not seen for years, and of whose private life I knew nothing. We were naturally very pleased to meet again, and on my invitation he accompanied us to a café, where we spent about two hours in pleasant conversation. To my question as to whether he was married he gave a negative answer, and added, 'Why should a man like me marry?'

"On leaving the café, he suddenly turned to me and said: 'I should like to know what you would do in a case like this: I know a nurse who was named as co-respondent in a divorce case. The wife sued the husband for divorce and named her as co-respondent, and *he* got the divorce.' I interrupted him, saying, 'You mean *she* got the divorce.' He immediately corrected himself, saying, 'Yes, she got the divorce,' and continued to tell how the excitement of the trial had affected this nurse to such an extent that she became nervous and took to drink. He wanted me to advise him how to treat her.

"As soon as I had corrected his mistake I asked him to explain it, but, as is usually the case, he was surprised at my question. He wanted to know whether a person had no right to make mistakes in talking. I explained to him that there is a reason for every mistake, and that if he had not told me that he was unmarried, I would say that he was the hero of the divorce case in question, and that the mistake showed that he wished he had obtained the divorce instead of his wife, so as not to be obliged to pay alimony and to be permitted to marry again in New York State.

"He stoutly denied my interpretation, but his emotional agitation, followed by loud laughter, only strengthened my suspicions. To my appeal that he should tell the truth 'for science' sake,' he said, 'Unless you wish me to lie you must believe that I was never married, and hence your psychoanalytic interpretation is all wrong.' He, however, added that it was dangerous to be with a person who paid attention to such little things. Then he suddenly remembered that he had another appointment and left us.

"Both Dr. Frink and I were convinced that my interpretation of his *lapsus linguæ* was correct, and I decided to corroborate or disprove it by further investigation. The next day I found a neighbour and old friend of Dr. P., who confirmed my interpretation in every particular. The divorce was granted to Dr. P.'s wife a few weeks before, and a nurse was named as co-respondent. A few weeks later I met Dr. P., and he told me that he was thoroughly convinced of the Freudian mechanisms."

The self-betrayal is just as plain in the following case reported by Otto Rank:—

A father who was devoid of all patriotic feeling and desirous of educating his children to be just as free from this superfluous sentiment, reproached his sons for participating in a patriotic demonstration, and rejected their reference to a similar behaviour of their uncle with these words: "You are not obliged to imitate him; why, he is an *idiot*." The astonished features of the children at their father's unusual tone aroused him to the fact that he had made a mistake, and he remarked apologetically, "Of course, I wished to say *patriot*."

When such a speech-blunder occurs in a serious squabble and reverses the intended meaning of one of the disputants, at once it puts him at a disadvantage with his adversary—a disadvantage which the latter seldom fails to utilize.

This clearly shows that although people are unwilling to accept the theory of my conception and are not inclined to forego the convenience that is connected with the tolerance of a faulty action, they nevertheless interpret speech-blunders and other faulty acts in a manner similar to the one presented in this book. The merriment and derision which are sure to be evoked at the decisive moment through such linguistic mistakes speak conclusively against the generally accepted convention that such a speech-blunder is a *lapsus linguæ* and psychologically of no importance. It was no less a man than the German Chancellor, Prince Bülow, who endeavoured to save the situation through such a protest when the wording of his defence of his Emperor (November, 1907) turned into the opposite through a speech-blunder.

"Concerning the present, the new epoch of Emperor Wilhelm II, I can only repeat what I said a year ago, that *it would be unfair and unjust to speak of a coterie of responsible advisers around our Emperor* (loud calls, 'Irresponsible!')—to speak of *irresponsible* advisers. Pardon the *lapsus linguæ*" (hilarity).

A nice example of speech-blunder, which aims not so much at the betrayal of the speaker as at the enlightenment of the listener outside the scene, is found in Wallenstein (*Piccolomini*, Act I, Scene 5), and shows us that the poet who here uses this means is well versed in the mechanism and intent of speech-blunders. In the preceding scene Max Piccolomini was passionately in favour of the ducal party, and was enthusiastic over the blessings of the peace which became known to him in the course of a journey while accompanying Wallenstein's daughter to the encampment. He leaves his father and the Court ambassador, Questenberg, in great consternation. The scene proceeds as follows:—

> QUESTENBERG. Woe unto us! Are matters thus? Friend, should we allow him to go there with this false opinion, and not recall him at once in order to open his eyes instantly.
> OCTAVIO (*rousing himself from profound meditation*). He has already opened mine, and I see more than pleases me.
> QUESTENBERG. What is it, friend?
> OCTAVIO. A curse on that journey!
> QUESTENBERG. Why? What is it?
> OCTAVIO. Come! I must immediately follow the unlucky trail, must see with my own eyes—come——(*Wishes to lead him away.*)
> QUESTENBERG. What is the matter? Where?
> OCTAVIO (*urging*). To *her*!
> QUESTENBERG. To——?
> OCTAVIO (*corrects himself*). To the duke! Let us go, etc.

The slight speech-blunder *to her* in place of *to him* is meant to betray to us the fact that the father has seen through his son's motive for espousing the other cause, while the courtier complains that "he speaks to him altogether in riddles."

Another example wherein a poet makes use of a speech-blunder was discovered by Otto Rank in Shakespeare. I quote Rank's report from the *Zentralblatt für Psychoanalyse*, I. 3.

"A poetic speech-blunder, very delicately motivated and technically remarkably well utilized, which, like the one pointed out by Freud in Wallenstein (*Zur Psychopathologie des Alltagslebens*, 2nd Edition, p. 48), not only shows that poets knew the mechanism and sense of this error, but also presupposes an understanding of it on the part of the hearer, can be found in Shakespeare's *Merchant of Venice* (Act III, Scene 2). By the will of her father, Portia was bound to select a husband through a lottery. She escaped all her distasteful suitors by lucky chance. When she finally found in Bassanio the suitor after her own heart, she had cause to fear lest he, too, should draw the unlucky lottery. In the scene she would like to tell him that even if he chose the wrong casket, he might, nevertheless, be sure of her love. But she is hampered by her vow. In this mental conflict the poet puts these words in her mouth, which were directed to the welcome suitor:—

> "There is something tells me (but it is not love),
> I would not lose you; and you know yourself
> Hate counsels not in such a quality.
> But lest you should not understand me well
> (And yet a maiden hath no tongue but thought),
> I would detain you here some month or two,
> Before you venture for me. I could teach you
> How to choose right, but then I am forsworn;
> So will I never be; so may you miss me;
> But if you do, you'll make me wish a sin,
> That I had been forsworn. Beshrew your eyes,
> They have o'erlooked me, and divided me:
> *One half of me is yours, the other half yours—*
> *Mine own, I would say*; but if mine, then yours—
> And so all yours."

"Just the very thing which she would like to hint to him gently, because really she should keep it from him, namely, that even before the choice she is wholly his—that she loves him, the poet, with admirable psychologic sensitiveness, allows to come to the surface in the speech-blunder. It is through this artifice that he manages to allay the intolerable uncertainty of the lover as well as the like tension of the hearer concerning the outcome of the choice."

The interest merited by the confirmation of our conception of speech-blunders through the great poets justifies the citation of a third example which was reported by Dr. E. Jones.[22]

"Our great novelist, George Meredith, in his masterpiece, *The Egoist*, shows an even finer understanding of the mechanism. The plot of the novel is, shortly, as follows: Sir Willoughby Patterne, an aristocrat greatly admired by his circle, becomes engaged to a Miss Constantia Durham. She discovers in him an intense egoism, which he skilfully conceals from the world, and to escape the marriage she elopes with a Captain Oxford. Some years later Patterne becomes engaged to a Miss Clara Middleton, and most of the book is taken up with a detailed description of the conflict that arises in her mind on also discovering his egoism. External circumstances and her conception of honour hold her to her pledge, while he becomes more and more distasteful in her eyes. She partly confided in his cousin and secretary, Vernon Whitford, the man whom she ultimately marries, but from a mixture of motives he stands aloof.

"In the soliloquy Clara speaks as follows: 'If some noble gentleman could see me as I am and not disdain to aid me! Oh! to be caught out of this prison of thorns and brambles. I cannot tear my own way out. I am a coward. A beckoning of a finger would change me, I believe. I could fly bleeding and through hootings to a comrade.... Constantia met a soldier. Perhaps she prayed and her prayer was answered. She did ill. But, oh, how I love her for it! His name was Harry Oxford.... She did not waver, she cut the links, she signed herself over. Oh, brave girl, what do you think of me? But I have no Harry Whitford; I am alone....' The sudden consciousness that she had put another name for Oxford struck her a buffet, drowning her in crimson.

"The fact that both men's names end in 'ford' evidently renders the confounding of them more easy, and would by many be regarded as an adequate cause for this, but the real underlying motive for it is plainly indicated by the author. In another passage the same *lapsus* occurs, and is followed by the hesitation and change of subject that one is familiar with in psychoanalysis when a half-conscious complex is touched. Sir Willoughby patronizingly says of Whitford: 'False alarm. The resolution to do anything unaccustomed is quite beyond poor old Vernon.' Clara replies: 'But if Mr. Oxford—Whitford ... your swans, coming sailing up the lake; how beautiful they look when they are indignant! I was going to ask you, surely men witnessing a marked admiration for some one else will naturally be discouraged?' Sir Willoughby stiffened with sudden enlightenment.

"In still another passage Clara, by another *lapsus*, betrays her secret wish that she was on a more intimate footing with Vernon Whitford. Speaking to a boy friend, she says, 'Tell Mr. Vernon—tell Mr. Whitford.'"

The conception of speech-blunders here defended can be readily verified in the smallest details. I have been able to demonstrate repeatedly that the most insignificant and most natural cases of speech-blunders have their good sense, and admit of the same interpretation as the more striking examples. A patient who, contrary to my wishes but with firm personal motives, decided upon a short trip to Budapest, justified herself by saying that she was going for only three days, but she blundered and said for only three weeks. She betrayed her secret feeling that, to spite me, she preferred spending three weeks to three days in that society which I considered unfit for her.

One evening, wishing to excuse myself for not having called for my wife at the theatre, I said: "I was at the theatre at ten minutes after ten." I was corrected: "You meant to say before ten o'clock." Naturally I wanted to say before ten. After ten would certainly be no excuse. I had been told that the theatre programme read, "Finished before ten o'clock." When I arrived at the theatre I found the foyer dark and the theatre empty. Evidently the performance was over earlier and my wife did not wait for me. When I looked at the clock it still wanted five minutes to ten. I determined to make my case more favourable at home, and say that it was ten minutes to ten. Unfortunately, the speech-blunder spoiled the intent and laid bare my dishonesty, in which I acknowledged more than there really was to confess.

This leads us to those speech disturbances which can no longer be described as speech-blunders, for they do not injure the individual word, but affect the rhythm and execution of the entire speech, as, for example, the stammering and stuttering of embarrassment. But here, as in the former cases, it is the inner conflict that is betrayed to us through the disturbance in speech. I really do not believe that any one will make mistakes in talking in an audience with His Majesty, in a serious love declaration, or in defending one's name and honour before a jury; in short, people make no mistakes where *they are all there*, as the saying goes. Even in criticizing an author's style we are allowed and accustomed to follow the principle of explanation, which we cannot miss in the origin of a single speech-blunder. A clear and unequivocal manner of writing shows us that here the author is in harmony with himself, but where we find a forced and involved expression, aiming at more than one target, as appropriately expressed, we can thereby recognize the participation of an unfinished and complicated thought, or we can hear through it the stifled voice of the author's self-criticism.[23]

***

VI

MISTAKES IN READING AND WRITING

That the same view-points and observation should hold true for mistakes in reading and writing as for lapses in speech is not at all surprising when one remembers the inner relation of these functions. I shall here confine myself to the reports of several carefully analysed examples and shall make no attempt to include all of the phenomena.

A. LAPSES IN READING.

(*a*) While looking over a number of the *Leipziger Illustrierten*, which I was holding obliquely, I read as the title of the front-page picture, "A Wedding Celebration in the Odyssey." Astonished and with my attention aroused, I moved the page into the proper position only to read correctly, "A Wedding Celebration in the Ostsee (Baltic Sea)." How did this senseless mistake in reading come about? Immediately my thoughts turned to a book by Ruth, *Experimental Investigations of "Music Phantoms"*, etc., with which I had recently been much occupied, as it closely touched the psychologic problems that are of interest to me. The author promised a work in the near future to be called *Analysis and Principles of Dream Phenomena.* No wonder that I, having just published an *Interpretation of Dreams*, awaited the appearance of this book with the most intense interest. In Ruth's work concerning music phantoms I found an announcement in the beginning of the table of contents of the detailed inductive proof that the old Hellenic myths and traditions originated mainly from slumber and music phantoms, from dream phenomena and from deliria. Thereupon I had immediately plunged into the text in order to find out whether he was also aware that the scene where Odysseus appears before Nausicaa was based upon the common dream of nakedness. One of my friends called my attention to the clever passage in G. Keller's *Grünem Heinrich*, which explains this episode in the Odyssey as an objective representation of the dream of the mariner straying far from home. I added to it the reference to the exhibition dream of nakedness.[24]

(*b*) A woman who is very anxious to get children always reads *storks* instead of *stocks*.

(*c*) One day I received a letter which contained very disturbing news. I immediately called my wife and informed her that poor Mrs. Wm. H. was seriously ill and was given up by the doctors. There must have been a false ring to the words in which I expressed my sympathy, as my wife grew suspicious, asked to see the letter, and expressed her opinion that it could not read as stated by me, because no one calls the wife by the husband's name. Moreover, the correspondent was well acquainted with the Christian name of the woman concerned. I defended my assertion obstinately and referred to the customary visiting-cards, on which a woman designates herself by the Christian name of her husband. I was finally compelled to take up the letter, and, as a matter of fact, we read therein "Poor W. M." What is more, I had even overlooked "Poor Dr. W. M." My mistake in reading signified a spasmodic effort, so to speak, to turn the sad news from the man towards the woman. The title between the adjective and the name did not go well with my claim that the woman must have been meant. That is why it was omitted in the reading. The motive for this falsifying was not that the woman was less an object of my sympathy than the man, but the fate of this poor man had excited my fears regarding another and nearer person who, I was aware, had the same disease.

(*d*) Both irritating and laughable is a lapse in reading to which I am frequently subject when I walk through the streets of a strange city during my vacation. I then read *antiquities* on every shop sign that shows the slightest resemblance to the word; this displays the questing spirit of the collector.

(*e*) In his important work[25] Bleuler relates: "While reading I once had the intellectual feeling of seeing my name two lines below. To my astonishment I found only the words blood corpuscles. Of the many thousands of lapses in reading in the peripheral as well as in the central field of vision that I have analysed, this was the most striking case. Whenever I imagined that I saw my name, the word that induced this illusion usually showed a greater resemblance to my name than the word *bloodcorpuscles*. In most cases all the letters of my name had to be close together before I could commit such an error. In this case, however, I could readily explain the delusion of reference and the illusion. What I had just read was the end of a statement concerning a form of bad style in scientific works, a tendency from which I am not entirely free."

B. LAPSES IN WRITING.

(*a*) On a sheet of paper containing principally short daily notes of business interest, I found, to my surprise, the incorrect date, "Thursday, October 20th," bracketed under the correct date of the month of September. It was not difficult to explain this anticipation as the expression of a wish. A few days before I had returned fresh from my vacation and felt ready for any amount of professional work, but as yet there were few patients. On my arrival I had found a letter from a patient announcing her arrival on the 20th of October. As I wrote the same date in September I may certainly have thought "X. ought to be here already; what a pity about that whole month!" and with this thought I pushed the current date a month ahead. In this case the disturbing thought can scarcely be called unpleasant; therefore after noticing this lapse in writing, I immediately knew the solution. In the fall of the following year I experienced an entirely analogous and similarly motivated lapse in writing. E. Jones has made a study of similar cases, and found that most mistakes in writing dates are motivated.

(*b*) I received the proof sheets of my contribution to the annual report on neurology and psychiatry, and I was naturally obliged to review with special care the names of authors, which, because of the many different nationalities represented, offer the greatest difficulties to the compositor. As a matter of fact, I found some strange-sounding names still in need of correction; but, oddly enough, the compositor had corrected one single name in my manuscript, and with very good reason. I had written *Buckrhard*, which the compositor guessed to be *Burckhard.* I had praised the treatise of this obstetrician entitled *The Influence of Birth on the Origin of Infantile Paralysis*, and I was not conscious of the least enmity toward him. But an author in Vienna, who had angered me by an adverse criticism of my *Traumdeutung*, bears the same name. It was as if in writing the name Burckhard, meaning the obstetrician, a wicked thought concerning the other B. had obtruded itself. The twisting of the name, as I have already stated in regard to lapses in speech, often signifies a depreciation.[26]

(*c*) The following is seemingly a serious case of *lapsus calami*, which it would be equally correct to describe as an erroneously carried out action. I intended to withdraw from the postal savings bank the sum of 300 crowns, which I wished to send to an absent relative to enable him to take treatment at a watering-place. I noted that my account was 4,380 crowns, and I decided to bring it down to the round sum of 4,000 crowns, which was not to be touched in the near future. After making out the regular cheque I suddenly noticed that I had written not 380 crowns, as I had intended, but exactly 438 crowns. I was frightened at the untrustworthiness of my action. I soon realized that my fear was groundless, as I had not grown poorer than I was before. But I had to reflect for quite a while in order to discover what influence diverted me from my first intention without making itself known to my consciousness. First I got on a wrong track: I subtracted 380 from 438, but after that I did not know what to do with the difference. Finally an idea occurred to me which showed me the true connection. 438 is exactly 10 per cent. of the entire account of 4,380 crowns! But the bookseller, too, gives a 10 per cent. discount! I recalled that a few days before I had selected several books, in which I was no longer interested, in order to offer them to the bookseller for 300 crowns. He thought the price demanded too high, but promised to give me a final answer within the next few days. If he should accept my first offer he would replace the exact sum that I was to spend on the sufferer. There is no doubt that I was sorry about this expenditure. The emotion at the realization of my mistakes can be more easily understood as a fear of growing poor through such outlays. But both the sorrow over this expense and the fear of poverty connected with it were entirely foreign to my consciousness; I did not regret this expense when I promised the sum, and would have laughed at the idea of any such underlying motive. I should probably not have assigned such feelings to myself had not my psychoanalytic practice made me quite familiar with the repressed elements of psychic life, and if I had not had a dream a few days before which brought forth the same solution.

(*d*) Although it is usually difficult to find the person responsible for printers' errors, the psychologic mechanisms underlying them are the same as in other mistakes. Typographical errors also well demonstrate the fact that people are not at all indifferent to such trivialities as "mistakes," and, judging by the indignant reactions of the parties concerned, one is forced to the conclusion that mistakes are not treated by the public at large as mere accidents. This state of affairs is very well summed up in the following editorial from the *New York Times* of April 14, 1913. Not the least interesting are the comments of the keen-witted editor, who seems to share our views:—

"A BLUNDER TRULY UNFORTUNATE.

"Typographical errors come only too frequently from even the best-regulated newspaper presses. They are always humiliating, often a cause of anger, and occasionally dangerous, but now and then they are distinctly amusing. This latter quality they are most apt to have when they are made in the office of a journalistic neighbour, a fact that probably explains why we can read with smiling composure an elaborate editorial apology which appears in the *Hartford Courant.*

"Its able political commentator tried the other day to say that, *unfortunately* for Connecticut, 'J. H. is no longer a Member of Congress. Printer and proof-reader combined to deprive the adverb of its negative particle.' At least, the able political commentator so declares, and we wouldn't question his veracity for the world; but sorrowful experience has taught most of us that it's safer to get that sort of editorial disclaimer of responsibility into print before looking up the copy, and perhaps—just perhaps—the world-enlightener, who *knows* that he wrote *unfortunate*, because that is what he intended to write, didn't rashly chance the discovery of his own guilt before he convicted the composing-room of it.

"Be that as it may, the meaning of the sentence was cruelly changed, and a friend was grieved or offended. Not so long ago a more astonishing error than this one crept into a book review of ours—a very solemn and scientific book. It consisted of the substitution of the word 'caribou' for the word 'carbon' in a paragraph dealing with the chemical composition of the stars. In that case the writer's fierce self-exculpation is at least highly plausible, as it seems hardly possible that he wrote 'caribou' when he intended to write 'carbon,' but even he was cautious enough to make no deep inquiry into the matter."

(*e*) I cite the following case contributed by Dr. W. Stekel, for the authenticity of which I can vouch: "An almost unbelievable example of miswriting and misreading occurred in the editing of a widely circulated weekly. It concerned an article of defence and vindication which was written with much warmth and great pathos. The editor-in-chief of the paper read the article, while the author himself naturally read it from the manuscript and proof-sheets more than once. Everybody was satisfied, when the printer's reader suddenly noticed a slight error which had escaped the attention of all. There it was, plainly enough: 'Our readers will bear witness to the fact that we have always acted in a *selfish* manner for the good of the community.' It is quite evident that it was meant to read *unselfish*. The real thoughts, however, broke through the pathetic speech with elemental force."

(*f*) The following example of misprinting is taken from a Western gazette: The teacher was giving an instruction paper on mathematical methods, and spoke of a plan "for the instruction of youth that might be carried out *ad libidinem*."

(*g*) Even the Bible did not escape misprints. Thus we have the "Wicked Bible," so called from the fact that the negative was left out of the seventh commandment. This authorized edition of the Bible was published in London in 1631, and it is said that the printer had to pay a fine of two thousand pounds for the omission. Another biblical misprint dates back to the year 1580, and is found in the Bible of the famous library of Wolfenbuttel, in Hesse. In the passage in Genesis where God tells Eve that Adam shall be her master and shall rule over her, the German translation is "*Und er soll dein Herr sein.*" The word *Herr* (master) was substituted by *Narr*, which means fool. Newly discovered evidence seems to show that the error was a conscious machination of the printer's suffragette wife, who refused to be ruled by her husband.

(*h*) Dr. Ernest Jones reports the following case concerning A. A. Brill: "Although by custom almost a teetotaler, he yielded to a friend's importunity one evening, in order to avoid offending him, and took a little wine. During the next morning an exacerbation of an eye-strain headache gave him cause to regret this slight indulgence, and his reflection on the subject found expression in the following slip of the pen. Having occasion to write the name of a girl mentioned by a patient, he wrote not Ethel but Ethyl.[27] It happened that the girl in question was rather too fond of drink, and in Dr. Brill's mood at the time this characteristic of hers stood out with conspicuous significance."[28]

(*i*) A woman wrote to her sister, felicitating her on the occasion of taking possession of a new and spacious residence. A friend who was present noticed that the writer put the wrong address on the letter, and what was still more remarkable was the fact that she did not address it to the previous residence, but to one long ago given up, but which her sister had occupied when she first married. When the friend called her attention to it the writer remarked, "You are right; but what in the world made me do this?" to which her friend replied: "Perhaps you begrudge her the nice big apartment into which she has just moved because you yourself are cramped for space, and for that reason you put her back into her first residence, where she was no better off than yourself." "Of course I begrudge her the new apartment," she honestly admitted. As an afterthought she added, "It is a pity that one is so mean in such matters."

(*k*) Ernest Jones reports the following example given to him by Dr. A. A. Brill. In a letter to Dr. Brill a patient tried to attribute his nervousness to business worries and excitement during the cotton crisis. He went on to say: "My trouble is all due to that d—— frigid wave; there isn't even any seed to be obtained for new crops." He referred to a cold wave which had destroyed the cotton crops, but instead of writing "wave" he wrote "wife." In the bottom of his heart he entertained reproaches against his wife on account of her marital frigidity and childlessness, and he was not far from the cognition that the enforced abstinence played no little part in the causation of his malady.

Omissions in writing are naturally explained in the same manner as mistakes in writing. A remarkable example of omission which is of historic importance was reported by Dr. B. Dattner.[29] In one of the legal articles dealing with the financial obligations of both countries, which was drawn up in the year 1867 during the readjustment between Austria and Hungary, the word "effective" was accidentally omitted in the Hungarian translation. Dattner thinks it probable that the unconscious desire of the Hungarian law-makers to grant Austria the least possible advantages had something to do with this omission.

Another example of omission is the following related by Brill: "A prospective patient, who had corresponded with me relative to treatment, finally wrote for an appointment for a certain day. Instead of keeping his appointment he sent regrets which began as follows: 'Owing to *foreseen* circumstances I am unable to keep my appointment.' He naturally meant to write *unforeseen*. He finally came to me months later, and in the course of the analysis I discovered that my suspicions at the time were justified; there were no unforeseen circumstances to prevent his coming at that time; he was advised not to come to me. The unconscious does not lie."

Wundt gives a most noteworthy proof for the easily ascertained fact that we more easily make mistakes in writing than in speaking (*loc. cit.*, p. 374). He states: "In the course of normal conversation the inhibiting function of the will is constantly directed toward bringing into harmony the course of ideation with the movement of articulation. If the articulation following the ideas becomes retarded through mechanical causes, as in writing, such anticipations then readily make their appearance."

Observation of the determinants which favour lapses in reading gives rise to doubt, which I do not like to leave unmentioned, because I am of the opinion that it may become the starting-point of a fruitful investigation. It is a familiar fact that in reading aloud the attention of the reader often wanders from the text and is directed toward his own thoughts. The results of this deviation of attention are often such that when interrupted and questioned he cannot even state what he has read. In other words, he has read automatically, although the reading was nearly always correct. I do not think that such conditions favour any noticeable increase in the mistakes. We are accustomed to assume concerning a whole series of functions that they are most precisely performed when done automatically, with scarcely any conscious attention. This argues that the conditions governing attention in mistakes in speaking, writing, and reading must be differently determined than assumed by Wundt (cessation or diminution of attention). The examples which we have subjected to analysis have really not given us the right to take for granted a quantitative diminution of attention. We found what is probably not exactly the same thing, a disturbance of the attention through a strange obtruding thought.

***

VII

FORGETTING OF IMPRESSIONS AND RESOLUTIONS

If any one should be inclined to overrate the state of our present knowledge of mental life, all that would be needed to force him to assume a modest attitude would be to remind him of the function of memory. No psychologic theory has yet been able to account for the connection between the fundamental phenomena of remembering and forgetting; indeed, even the complete analysis of that which one can actually observe has as yet scarcely been grasped. To-day forgetting has perhaps grown more puzzling than remembering, especially since we have learned from the study of dreams and pathologic states that even what for a long time we believed forgotten may suddenly return to consciousness.

To be sure, we are in possession of some view-points which we hope will receive general recognition. Thus we assume that forgetting is a spontaneous process to which we may ascribe a certain temporal discharge. We emphasize the fact that, just as among the units of every impression or experience, in forgetting, too, a certain selection takes place among the existing impressions. We are acquainted with some of the conditions that underlie the tenaciousness of memory and the awakening of that which would otherwise remain forgotten. Nevertheless, we can observe in innumerable cases of daily life how unreliable and unsatisfactory our knowledge of the mechanism is. Thus we may listen to two persons exchanging reminiscences concerning the same outward impressions, say of a journey that they have taken together some time before. What remains most firmly in the memory of the one is often forgotten by the other, as if it had never occurred, even when there is not the slightest reason to assume that this impression is of greater psychic importance for the one than for the other. A great many of those factors which determine the selective power of memory are obviously still beyond our ken.

With the purpose of adding some small contribution to the knowledge of the conditions of forgetting, I was wont to subject to a psychologic analysis those cases in which forgetting concerned me personally. As a rule I took up only a certain group of those cases, namely, those in which the forgetting astonished me, because, in my opinion, I should have remembered the experience in question. I wish further to remark that I am generally not inclined to forgetfulness (of things experienced, not of things learned), and that for a short period of my youth I was able to perform extraordinary feats of memory. When I was a schoolboy it was quite natural for me to be able to repeat from memory the page of a book which I had read; and shortly before I entered the University I could write down practically verbatim the popular lectures on scientific subjects directly after hearing them. In the tension before the final medical examination I must have made use of the remnant of this ability, for in certain subjects I gave the examiners apparently automatic answers, which proved to be exact reproductions of the text-book, which I had skimmed through but once and then in greatest haste.

Since those days I have steadily lost control over my memory; of late, however, I became convinced that with the aid of a certain artifice I can recall far more than I would otherwise credit myself with remembering. For example, when, during my office hours, a patient states that I have seen him before and I cannot recall either the fact or the time, then I help myself by guessing—that is, I allow a number of years, beginning from the present time, to come to my mind quickly. Whenever this could be controlled by records of definite information from the patient, it was always shown that in over ten years[30] I have seldom missed it by more than six months. The same thing happens when I meet a casual acquaintance and, from politeness, inquire about his small child. When he tells of its progress I try to fancy how old the child now is. I control my estimate by the information given by the father, and at most I make a mistake of a month, and in older children of three months. I cannot state, however, what basis I have for this estimate. Of late I have grown so bold that I always offer my estimate spontaneously, and still run no risk of grieving the father by displaying my ignorance in regard to his offspring. Thus I extend my conscious memory by invoking my larger unconscious memory.

I shall report some *striking* examples of forgetting which for the most part I have observed in myself. I distinguish forgetting of impressions and experiences, that is, the forgetting of knowledge, from forgetting of resolutions, that is, the forgetting of omissions. The uniform result of the entire series of observations I can formulate as follows: *The forgetting in all cases is proved to be founded on a motive of displeasure.*

A. FORGETTING OF IMPRESSIONS AND KNOWLEDGE.

(*a*) During the summer my wife once made me very angry, although the cause in itself was trifling. We sat in a restaurant opposite a gentleman from Vienna whom I knew, and who had cause to know me, and whose acquaintance I had reasons for not wishing to renew. My wife, who had heard nothing to the disrepute of the man opposite her, showed by her actions that she was listening to his conversation with his neighbours, for from time to time she asked me questions which took up the thread of their discussion. I became impatient and finally irritated. A few weeks later I complained to a relative about this behaviour on the part of my wife, but I was not able to recall even a single word of the conversation of the gentleman in the case. As I am usually rather resentful and cannot forget a single incident of an episode that has annoyed me, my amnesia in this case was undoubtedly determined by respect for my wife. A short time ago I had a similar experience. I wished to make merry with an intimate friend over a statement made by my wife only a few hours earlier, but I found myself hindered by the noteworthy fact that I had entirely forgotten the statement. I had first to beg my wife to recall it to me. It is easy to understand that my forgetting in this case may be analogous to the typical disturbance of judgment which dominates us when it concerns those nearest to us.

(*b*) To oblige a woman who was a stranger in Vienna I had undertaken to procure a small iron safe for the preservation of documents and money. When I offered my services, the image of an establishment in the heart of the city where I was sure I had seen such safes floated before me with extraordinary visual vividness. To be sure, I could not recall the name of the street, but I felt certain that I would discover the store in a walk through the city, for my memory told me that I had passed it countless times. To my chagrin I could not find this establishment with the safes, though I walked through the inner part of the city in every direction. I concluded that the only thing left to do was to search through a business directory, and if that failed, to try to identify the establishment in a second round of the city. It did not, however, require so much effort; among the addresses in the directory I found one which immediately presented itself as that which had been forgotten. It was true that I had passed the show window countless times, each time, however, when I had gone to visit the M. family, who have lived a great many years in this identical building. After this intimate friendship had turned to an absolute estrangement, I had taken care to avoid the neighbourhood as well as the house, though without ever thinking of the reason for my action. In my walk through the city searching for the safe in the show window I had traversed every street in the neighbourhood but the right one, and I had avoided this as if it were forbidden ground. The motive of displeasure which was at the bottom of my disorientation is thus comprehensible. But the mechanism of forgetting is no longer so simple as in the former example. Here my aversion naturally does not extend to the vendor of safes, but to another person, concerning whom I wish to know nothing, and later transfers itself from the latter to this incident where it brings about the forgetting. Similarly, in the case of *Burckhard* mentioned above, the grudge against the one brought about the error in writing the name of the other. The similarity of names which here established a connection between two essentially different streams of thought was accomplished in the showcase window instance by the contiguity of space and the inseparable environment. Moreover, this latter case was more closely knit together, for money played a great part in the causation of the estrangement from the family living in this house.

(*c*) The B. and R. Company requested me to pay a professional call on one of their officers. On my way to him I was engrossed in the thought that I must already have been in the building occupied by the firm. It seemed as if I used to see their signboard in a lower story while my professional visit was taking me to a higher story. I could not recall, however, which house it was nor when I had called there. Although the entire matter was indifferent and of no consequence, I nevertheless occupied myself with it, and at last learned in the usual roundabout way, by collecting the thoughts that occurred to me in this connection, that one story above the floor occupied by the firm B. and R. was the *Pension Fischer*, where I had frequently visited patients. Then I remembered the building which sheltered both the company and the *pension*. I was still puzzled, however, as to the motive that entered into play in this forgetting. I found nothing disagreeable in my memory concerning the firm itself or the *Pension Fischer*, or the patients living there. I was also aware that it could not deal with anything very painful, otherwise I hardly would have been successful in tracing the thing forgotten in a roundabout way without resorting to external aid, as happened in the preceding example. Finally it occurred to me that a little before, while starting on my way to a new patient, a gentleman whom I had difficulty in recalling greeted me in the street. Some months previously I had seen this man in an apparently serious condition and had made the diagnosis of general paresis, but later I had learned of his recovery, consequently my judgment had been incorrect. Was it not possible that we had in this case a remission, which one usually finds in *dementia paralytica*? In that contingency my diagnosis would still be justified. The influence emanating from this meeting caused me to forget the neighbourhood of the B. and R. Company, and my interest to discover the thing forgotten was transferred from this case of disputed diagnosis. But the associative connection in this loose inner relation was effected by means of a similarity of names: the man who recovered, contrary to expectation, was also an officer of a large company that recommends patients to me. And the physician with whom I had seen the supposed paretic bore the name of Fischer, the name of the *pension* in the house which I had forgotten.

(*d*) Mislaying a thing really has the same significance as forgetting where we have placed it. Like most people delving in pamphlets and books, I am well oriented about my desk, and can produce what I want with one lunge. What appears to others as disorder has become for me perfect order. Why, then, did I mislay a catalogue which was sent to me not long ago so that it could not be found? What is more, it had been my intention to order a book which I found announced therein, entitled *Ueber die Sprache*, because it was written by an author whose spirited, vivacious style I like, whose insight into psychology and whose knowledge of the cultural world I have learned to appreciate. I believe that was just why I mislaid the catalogue. It was my habit to lend the books of this author among my friends for their enlightenment, and a few days before, on returning one, somebody had said: "His style reminds me altogether of yours, and his way of thinking is identical." The speaker did not know what he was stirring up with this remark. Years ago, when I was younger and in greater need of forming alliances, I was told practically the same thing by an older colleague, to whom I had recommended the writings of a familiar medical author. To put it in his words, "It is absolutely your style and manner." I was so influenced by these remarks that I wrote a letter to this author with the object of bringing about a closer relation, but a rather cool answer put me back "in my place." Perhaps still earlier discouraging experiences conceal themselves behind this last one, for I did not find the mislaid catalogue. Through this premonition I was actually prevented from ordering the advertised book, although the disappearance of the catalogue formed no real hindrance, as I remembered well both the name of the book and the author.

(*e*) Another case of mislaying merits our interest on account of the conditions under which the mislaid object was rediscovered. A younger man narrates as follows: "Several years ago there were some misunderstandings between me and my wife. I found her too cold, and though I fully appreciated her excellent qualities, we lived together without evincing any tenderness for each other. One day on her return from a walk she gave me a book which she had bought because she thought it would interest me. I thanked her for this mark of 'attention,' promised to read the book, put it away, and did not find it again. So months passed, during which I occasionally remembered the lost book, and also tried in vain to find it. "About six months later my beloved mother, who was not living with us, became ill. My wife left home to nurse her mother-in-law. The patient's condition became serious and gave my wife the opportunity to show the best side of herself. One evening I returned home full of enthusiasm over what my wife had accomplished, and felt very grateful to her. I stepped to my desk and, without definite intention but with the certainty of a somnambulist, I opened a certain drawer, and in the very top of it I found the long-missing, mislaid book." The following example of "misplacing" belongs to a type well known to every psychoanalyst. I must add that the patient who experienced this misplacing has himself found the solution of it. This patient, whose psychoanalytic treatment had to be interrupted through the summer vacation when he was in a state of resistance and ill-health, put away his keys in the evening in their usual place, or so he thought. He then remembered that he wished to take some things from his desk, where he also had put the money which he needed on the journey. He was to depart the next day, which was the last day of treatment and the date when the doctor's fee was due. But the keys had disappeared. He began a thorough and systematic search through his small apartment. He became more and more excited over it, but his search was unsuccessful. As he recognized this "misplacement" as a symptomatic act—that is, as being intentional—he aroused his servant in order to continue his search with the help of an "unprejudiced" person. After another hour he gave up the search and feared that he had lost the keys. The next morning he ordered new keys from the desk factory, which were hurriedly made for him. Two acquaintances who had been with him in a cab even recalled hearing something fall to the ground as he stepped out of the cab, and he was therefore convinced that the keys had slipped from his pocket. They were found lying between a thick book and a thin pamphlet, the latter a work of one of my pupils, which he wished to take along as reading matter for his vacation; and they were so skilfully placed that no one would have supposed that they were there. He himself was unable to replace the keys in such a position as to render them invisible. The unconscious skill with which an object is misplaced on account of secret but strong motives reminds one of "somnambulistic sureness." The motive was naturally ill-humour over the interruption of the treatment and the secret rage over the fact that he had to pay such a high fee when he felt so ill.

(*f*) Brill relates:[31] "A man was urged by his wife to attend a social function in which he really took no interest. Yielding to his wife's entreaties, he began to take his dress-suit from the trunk when he suddenly thought of shaving. After accomplishing this he returned to the trunk and found it locked. Despite a long, earnest search the key could not be found. A locksmith could not be found on Sunday evening, so that the couple had to send their regrets. On having the trunk opened the next morning the lost key was found within. The husband had absent-mindedly dropped the key into the trunk and sprung the lock. He assured me that this was wholly unintentional and unconscious, but we know that he did not wish to go to this social affair. The mislaying of the key therefore lacked no motive." Ernest Jones noticed in himself that he was in the habit of mislaying his pipe whenever he suffered from the effects of over-smoking. The pipe was then found in some unusual place where it did not belong and which it normally did not occupy. If one looks over the cases of mislaying it will be difficult to assume that mislaying is anything other than the result of an unconscious intention.

(*g*) In the summer of 1901 I once remarked to a friend with whom I was then actively engaged in exchanging ideas on scientific questions: "These neurotic problems can be solved only if we take the position of absolutely accepting an original bi-sexuality in every individual." To which he replied: "I told you that two and a half years ago while we were taking an evening walk in Br. At that time you wouldn't listen to it."

It is truly painful to be thus requested to renounce one's originality. I could neither recall such a conversation nor my friend's revelation. One of us must be mistaken; and according to the principle of the question *cui prodest?* I must be the one. Indeed, in the course of the following weeks everything came back to me just as my friend had recalled it. I myself remembered that at that time I gave the answer: "I have not yet got so far, and I do not care to discuss it." But since this incident I have grown more tolerant when I miss any mention of my name in medical literature in connection with ideas for which I deserve credit.

It is scarcely accidental that the numerous examples of forgetting which have been collected without any selection should require for their solution the introduction of such painful themes as exposing of one's wife; a friendship that has turned into the opposite; a mistake in medical diagnosis; enmity on account of similar pursuits, or the borrowing of somebody's ideas. I am rather inclined to believe that every person who will undertake an inquiry into the motives underlying his forgetting will be able to fill up a similar sample card of vexatious circumstances. The tendency to forget the disagreeable seems to me to be quite general; the capacity for it is naturally differently developed in different persons. Certain *denials* which we encounter in medical practice can probably be ascribed to *forgetting*.[32] Our conception of such forgetting confines the distinction between this and that behaviour to purely psychologic relations, and permits us to see in both forms of reaction the expression of the same motive. Of the numerous examples of denials of unpleasant recollection which I have observed in kinsmen of patients, one remains in my memory as especially singular.

A mother telling me of the childhood of her nervous son, now in his puberty, made the statement that, like his brothers and sisters, he was subject to bed-wetting throughout his childhood, a symptom which certainly has some significance in a history of a neurotic patient. Some weeks later, while seeking information regarding the treatment, I had occasion to call her attention to signs of a constitutional morbid predisposition in the young man, and at the same time referred to the bed-wetting recounted in the anamnesis. To my surprise she contested this fact concerning him, denying it as well for the other children, and asked me how I could possibly know this. Finally I let her know that she herself had told me a short time before what she had thus forgotten.[33]

One also finds abundant indications which show that even in healthy, not neurotic, persons resistances are found against the memory of disagreeable impressions and the idea of painful thoughts.[34] But the full significance of this fact can be estimated only when we enter into the psychology of neurotic persons. One is forced to make such elementary defensive striving against ideas which can awaken painful feelings, a striving which can be put side by side only with the flight-reflex in painful stimuli, as the main pillar of the mechanism which carries the hysterical symptoms. One need not offer any objection to the acceptance of such defensive tendency on the ground that we frequently find it impossible to rid ourselves of painful memories which cling to us, or to banish such painful emotions as remorse and reproaches of conscience. No one maintains that this defensive tendency invariably gains the upper hand, that in the play of psychic forces it may not strike against factors which stir up the contrary feeling for other purposes and bring it about in spite of it.

As the architectural principle of the psychic apparatus we may conjecture a certain stratification or structure of instances deposited in strata. And it is quite possible that this defensive tendency belongs to a lower psychic instance, and is inhibited by higher instances. At all events, it speaks for the existence and force of this defensive tendency, when we can trace it to processes such as those found in our examples of forgetting. We see then that something is forgotten for its own sake, and where this is not possible the defensive tendency misses the target and causes something else to be forgotten—something less significant, but which has fallen into associative connection with the disagreeable material.

The views here developed, namely, that painful memories merge into motivated forgetting with special ease, merits application in many spheres where as yet it has found no, or scarcely any, recognition. Thus it seems to me that it has not yet been strongly enough emphasized in the estimation of testimony taken in court,[35] where the putting of a witness under oath obviously leads us to place too great a trust on the purifying influence of his psychic play of forces. It is universally admitted that in the origin of the traditions and folklore of a people care must be taken to eliminate from memory such a motive as would be painful to the national feeling. Perhaps on closer investigation it may be possible to form a perfect analogy between the manner of development of national traditions and infantile reminiscences of the individual. The great Darwin has formulated a "golden rule" for the scientific worker from his insight into this pain-motive of forgetting.[36]

Almost exactly as in the forgetting of names, faulty recollections can also appear in the forgetting of impressions, and when finding credence they may be designated as delusions of memory. The memory disturbance in pathologic cases (in paranoia it actually plays the rôle of a constituting factor in the formation of delusions) has brought to light an extensive literature in which there is no reference whatever to its being motivated. As this theme also belongs to the psychology of the neuroses it goes beyond our present treatment. Instead, I will give from my own experience a curious example of memory disturbance showing clearly enough its determination through unconscious repressed material and its connection with this material.

While writing the latter chapters of my volume on the interpretation of dreams, I happened to be in a summer resort without access to libraries and reference books, so that I was compelled to introduce into the manuscript all kinds of references and citations from memory. These I naturally reserved for future correction. In the chapter on day-dreams I thought of the distinguished figure of the poor book-keeper in Alphonse Daudet's *Nabab*, through whom the author probably described his own day-dreams. I imagined that I distinctly remembered one fantasy of this man, whom I called Mr. Jocelyn, which he hatched while walking the streets of Paris, and I began to reproduce it from memory. This fantasy described how Mr. Jocelyn boldly hurled himself at a runaway horse and brought it to a standstill; how the carriage door opened and a great personage stepped from the coupé, pressed Mr. Jocelyn's hand and said: "You are my saviour—I owe my life to you! What can I do for you?"

I assured myself that casual inaccuracies in the rendition of this fantasy could readily be corrected at home on consulting the book. But when I perused *Nabab* in order to compare it with my manuscript, I found to my very great shame and consternation that there was nothing to suggest such a dream by Mr. Jocelyn; indeed, the poor book-keeper did not even bear this name—he was called Mr. Joyeuse.

This second error then furnished the key for the solution of the first mistake, the faulty reminiscence. Joyeux, of which Joyeuse is the feminine form, was the only possible word which would translate my own name *Freud* into French. Whence, therefore, came this falsely remembered fantasy which I had attributed to Daudet? It could only be a product of my own, a day-dream which I myself had spun, and which did not become conscious, or which was once conscious and had since been absolutely forgotten. Perhaps I invented it myself in Paris, where frequently enough I walked the streets alone, and full of longing for a helper and protector, until Charcot took me into his circle. I had often met the author of *Nabab* in Charcot's house. But the provoking part of it all is the fact that there is scarcely anything to which I am so hostile as the thought of being some one's protégé. What we see of this sort of thing in our country spoils all desire for it, and my character is little suited to the rôle of a protected child. I have always entertained an immense desire to "be the strong man myself." And it had to happen that I should be reminded of such a, to be sure, never fulfilled, day-dream! Besides, this incident is a good example of how the restraint relation to one's ego, which breaks forth triumphantly in paranoia, disturbs and entangles us in the objective grasp of things.

Another case of faulty recollection which can be satisfactorily explained resembles the *fausse reconnaissance* to be discussed later. I related to one of my patients, an ambitious and very capable man, that a young student had recently gained admittance into the circle of my pupils by means of an interesting work, *Der Künstler, Versuch einer Sexualpsychologie*. When, a year and a quarter later, this work lay before me in print, my patient maintained that he remembered with certainty having read somewhere, perhaps in a bookseller's advertisement, the announcement of the same book even before I first mentioned it to him. He remembered that this announcement came to his mind at that time, and he ascertained besides that the author had changed the title, that it no longer read "*Versuch*" but "*Ansätze zu einer Sexualpsychologie*."

Careful inquiry of the author and comparison of all dates showed conclusively that my patient was trying to recall the impossible. No notice of this work had appeared anywhere before its publication, certainly not a year and a quarter before it went to print. However, I neglected to seek a solution for this false recollection until the same man brought about an equally valuable renewal of it. He thought that he had recently noticed a work on "agoraphobia" in the show window of a bookshop, and as he was now looking for it in all available catalogues I was able to explain to him why his effort must remain fruitless. The work on agoraphobia existed only in his fantasy as an unconscious resolution to write such a book himself. His ambition to emulate that young man, and through such a scientific work to become one of my pupils, had led him to the first as well as to the second false recollection. He also recalled later that the bookseller's announcement which had occasioned his false reminiscence dealt with a work entitled *Genesis, Das Gesetz der Zeugung* ("Genesis, The Law of Generation"). But the change in the title as mentioned by him was really instigated by me; I recalled that I myself have perpetrated the same inaccuracy in the repetition of the title by saying "*Ansätze*" in place of "*Versuch*."

B. FORGETTING OF INTENTIONS.

No other group of phenomena is better qualified to demonstrate the thesis that lack of attention does not in itself suffice to explain faulty acts as the forgetting of intentions. An intention is an impulse for an action which has already found approbation, but whose execution is postponed for a suitable occasion. Now, in the interval thus created sufficient change may take place in the motive to prevent the intention from coming to execution. It is not, however, forgotten, it is simply revised and omitted.

We are naturally not in the habit of explaining the forgetting of intentions which we daily experience in every possible situation as being due to a recent change in the adjustment of motives. We generally leave it unexplained, or we seek a psychologic explanation in the assumption that at the time of execution the required attention for the action, which was an indispensable condition for the occurrence of the intention, and was then at the disposal of the same action, no longer exists. Observation of our normal behaviour towards intentions urges us to reject this tentative explanation as arbitrary. If I resolve in the morning to carry out a certain intention in the evening, I may be reminded of it several times in the course of the day, but it is not at all necessary that it should become conscious throughout the day. As the time for its execution approaches it suddenly occurs to me and induces me to make the necessary preparation for the intended action. If I go walking and take a letter with me to be posted, it is not at all necessary that I, as a normal not nervous individual, should carry it in my hand and continually look for a letter-box. As a matter of fact I am accustomed to put it in my pocket and give my thoughts free rein on my way, feeling confident that the first letter-box will attract my attention and cause me to put my hand in my pocket and draw out the letter.

This normal behaviour in a formed intention corresponds perfectly with the experimentally produced conduct of persons who are under a so-called "post-hypnotic suggestion" to perform something after a certain time.[37] We are accustomed to describe the phenomenon in the following manner: the suggested intention slumbers in the person concerned until the time for its execution approaches. Then it awakes and excites the action.

In two positions of life even the layman is cognizant of the fact that forgetting referring to intended purposes can in no wise claim consideration as an elementary phenomenon no further reducible, but realizes that it ultimately depends on unadmitted motives. I refer to affairs of love and military service. A lover who is late at the appointed place will vainly tell his sweetheart that unfortunately he has entirely forgotten their rendezvous. She will not hesitate to answer him: "A year ago you would not have forgotten. Evidently you no longer care for me." Even if he should grasp the above cited psychologic explanation, and should wish to excuse his forgetting on the plea of important business, he would only elicit the answer from the woman, who has become as keen-sighted as the physician in the psychoanalytic treatment, "How remarkable that such business disturbances did not occur before!" Of course the woman does not wish to deny the possibility of forgetting; but she believes, and not without reason, that practically the same inference of a certain unwillingness may be drawn from the unintentional forgetting as from a conscious subterfuge.

Similarly, in military service no distinction is recognized between an omission resulting from forgetting and one in consequence of intentional neglect. And rightly so. The soldier dares forget nothing that military service demands of him. If he forgets in spite of this, even when he is acquainted with the demands, then it is due to the fact that the motives which urge the fulfilment of the military exactions are opposed by contrary motives. Thus the one year's volunteer[38] who at inspection pleads forgetting as an excuse for not having polished his buttons is sure to be punished. But this punishment is small in comparison to the one he courts if he admits to his superiors that the motive for his negligence is because "this miserable menial service is altogether disgusting to me." Owing to this saving of punishment for economic reasons, as it were, he makes use of forgetting as an excuse, or it comes about as a compromise.

The service of women (as well as the military service of the State) demands that nothing relating to that service be subject to forgetting. Thus it but suggests that forgetting is permissible in unimportant matters, but in weighty matters its occurrence is an indication that one wishes to treat weighty matters as unimportant: that is, that their importance is disputed.[39] The view-point of psychic validity is in fact not to be contested here. No person forgets to carry out actions that seem important to himself without exposing himself to the suspicion of being a sufferer from mental weakness. Our investigations therefore can extend only to the forgetting of more or less secondary intentions, for no intention do we deem absolutely indifferent, otherwise it would certainly never have been formed.

As in the preceding functional disturbances, I have collected the cases of neglect through forgetting which I have observed in myself, and endeavoured to explain them. I have found that they could invariably be traced to some interference of unknown and unadmitted motives—or, as may be said, they were due to a counter-will. In a number of these cases I found myself in a position similar to that of being in some distasteful service: I was under a constraint to which I had not entirely resigned myself, so that I showed my protest in the form of forgetting. This accounts for the fact that I am particularly prone to forget to send congratulations on such occasions as birthdays, jubilees, wedding celebrations, and promotions to higher rank. I continually make new resolutions, but I am more than ever convinced that I shall not succeed. I am now on the point of giving it up altogether, and to admit consciously the striving motives. In a period of transition, I told a friend who asked me to send a congratulatory telegram for him, at a certain time when I was to send one myself, that I would probably forget both. It was not surprising that the prophecy came true. It is undoubtedly due to painful experiences in life that I am unable to manifest sympathy where this manifestation must necessarily appear exaggerated, for the small amount of my feeling does not admit the corresponding expression. Since I have learned that I often mistook the pretended sympathy of others for real, I am in rebellion against the conventions of expressing sympathy, the social expediency of which I naturally acknowledge. Condolences in cases of death are excepted from this double treatment; once I determine to send them I do not neglect them. Where my emotional participation has nothing more to do with social duty, its expression is never inhibited by forgetting.

Cases in which we forget to carry out actions which we have promised to do as a favour for others can similarly be explained as antagonism to conventional duty and as an unfavourable inward opinion. Here it regularly proves correct, inasmuch as the only person appealed to believes in the excusing power of forgetfulness, while the one requesting the favour has no doubt about the right answer: he has no interest in this matter, otherwise he would not have forgotten it.

There are some who are noted as generally forgetful, and we excuse their lapses in the same manner as we excuse those who are short-sighted when they do not greet us in the street.[40] Such persons forget all small promises which they have made; they leave unexecuted all orders which they have received; they prove themselves unreliable in little things; and at the same time demand that we shall not take these slight offences amiss—that is, they do not want us to attribute these failings to personal characteristics but to refer them to an organic peculiarity.[41] I am not one of these people myself, and have had no opportunity to analyse the actions of such a person in order to discover from the selection of forgetting the motive underlying the same. I cannot forego, however, the conjecture *per analogiam*, that here the motive is an unusual large amount of unavowed disregard for others which exploits the constitutional factor for its purpose.[42]

In other cases the motives for forgetting are less easy to discover, and when found excite greater astonishment. Thus, in former years I observed that of a great number of professional calls I only forgot those that I was to make on patients whom I treated gratis or on colleagues. The mortification caused by this discovery led me to the habit of noting every morning the calls of the day in a form of resolution. I do not know if other physicians have come to the same practice by a similar road. Thus we get an idea of what causes the so-called neurasthenic to make a memorandum of the communications he wishes to make to the doctor. He apparently lacks confidence in the reproductive capacity of his memory. This is true, but the scene usually proceeds in this manner. The patient has recounted his various complaints and inquiries at considerable length. After he has finished he pauses for a moment, then he pulls out the memorandum and says apologetically, "I have made some notes because I cannot remember anything." As a rule he finds nothing new on the memorandum. He repeats each point and answers it himself: "Yes, I have already asked about that." By means of the memorandum he probably only demonstrates one of his symptoms, the frequency with which his resolutions are disturbed through the interference of obscure motives.

I am touching, moreover, on an affliction to which even most of my healthy acquaintances are subject, when I admit that especially in former years I had the habit of easily forgetting for a long time to return borrowed books, also that it very often happened that I deferred payments through forgetfulness. One morning not long ago I left the tobacco-shop where I make my daily purchase of cigars without paying. It was a most harmless omission, as I am known there and could therefore expect to be reminded of my debt the next morning. But this slight neglect, the attempt to contract a debt, was surely not unconnected with reflections concerning the budget with which I had occupied myself throughout the preceding day. Even among the so-called respectable people one can readily demonstrate a double behaviour when it concerns the theme of money and possession. The primitive greed of the suckling which wishes to seize every object (in order to put it in its mouth) has generally been only imperfectly subdued through culture and training.[43]

I fear that in all the examples thus far given I have grown quite commonplace. But it can be only a pleasure to me if I happen upon familiar matters which every one understands, for my main object is to collect everyday material and utilize it scientifically. I cannot conceive why wisdom, which is, so to speak, the sediment of everyday experiences, should be denied admission among the acquisitions of knowledge. For it is not the diversity of objects but the stricter method of verification and the striving for far-reaching connections which make up the essential character of scientific work.

We have invariably found that intentions of some importance are forgotten when obscure motives arise to disturb them. In still less important intentions we find a second mechanism of forgetting. Here a counter-will becomes transferred to the resolution from something else after an external association has been formed between the latter and the content of the resolution. The following example reported by Brill illustrates this: "A patient found that she had suddenly become very negligent in her correspondence. She was naturally punctual and took pleasure in letter-writing, but for the last few weeks she simply could not bring herself to write a letter without exerting the greatest amount of effort. The explanation was quite simple. Some weeks before she had received an important letter calling for a categorical answer. She was undecided what to say, and therefore did not answer it at all. This indecision in the form of inhibition was unconsciously transferred to other letters and caused the inhibition against letter-writing in general."

Direct counter-will and more remote motivation are found together in the following example of delaying: I had written a short treatise on the dream for the series *Grenzfragen des Nerven- und Seelenlebens*, in which I gave an abstract of my book, *The Interpretation of Dreams*.[44] Bergmann, the publisher, had sent me the proof sheets and asked for a speedy return of the same as he wished to issue the pamphlet before Christmas. I corrected the sheets the same night, and placed them on my desk in order to take them to the post office the next morning. In the morning I forgot all about it, and only thought of it in the afternoon at the sight of the paper cover on my desk. In the same way I forgot the proofs that evening and the following morning, and until the afternoon of the second day, when I quickly took them to a letter-box, wondering what might be the basis of this procrastination. Obviously I did not want to send them off, although I could find no explanation for such an attitude.

After posting the letter I entered the shop of my Vienna publisher, who put out my *Interpretation of Dreams*. I left a few orders; then, as if impelled by a sudden thought, said, "You undoubtedly know that I have written the 'Dream' book a second time?" "Ah!" he exclaimed, "then I must ask you to——" "Calm yourself," I interposed; "it is only a short treatise for the Löwenfeld-Kurella collection." But still he was not satisfied; he feared that the abstract would hurt the sale of the book. I disagreed with him, and finally asked: "If I had come to you before, would you have objected to the publication?" "No; under no circumstances," he answered.

Personally I believe I acted within my full rights and did nothing contrary to the general practice; still it seems certain to me that a thought similar to that entertained by the publisher was the motive for my procrastination in dispatching the proof sheets.

This reflection leads back to a former occasion when another publisher raised some difficulties because I was obliged to take out several pages of the text from an earlier work on cerebral infantile paralysis, and put them unchanged into a work on the same theme in Nothnagel's handbook. There again the reproach received no recognition; that time also I had loyally informed my first publisher (the same who published *The Interpretation of Dreams*) of my intention.

However, if this series of recollections is followed back still farther it brings to light a still earlier occasion relating to a translation from the French, in which I really violated the property rights that should be considered in a publication. I had added notes to the text without asking the author's permission, and some years later I had cause to think that the author was dissatisfied with this arbitrary action.

There is a proverb which indicates the popular knowledge that the forgetting of intentions is not accidental. It says: "What one forgets once he will often forget again."

Indeed, we sometimes cannot help feeling that no matter what may be said about forgetting and faulty actions, the whole subject is already known to everybody as something self-evident. It is strange enough that it is still necessary to push before consciousness such well-known facts. How often I have heard people remark: "Please do not ask me to do this, I shall surely forget it." The coming true of this prophecy later is surely nothing mysterious in itself. He who speaks thus perceives the inner resolution not to carry out the request, and only hesitates to acknowledge it to himself.

Much light is thrown, moreover, on the forgetting of resolutions through something which could be designated as "forming false resolutions." I had once promised a young author to write a review of his short work, but on account of inner resistances, not unknown to me, I promised him that it would be done the same evening. I really had serious intentions of doing so, but I had forgotten that I had set aside that evening for the preparation of an expert testimony that could not be deferred. After I thus recognized my resolution as false, I gave up the struggle against my resistances and refused the author's request.

***

VIII

ERRONEOUSLY CARRIED-OUT ACTIONS

I shall give another passage from the above-mentioned work of Meringer and Mayer (p. 98):

"Lapses in speech do not stand entirely alone. They resemble the errors which often occur in our other activities and are quite foolishly termed 'forgetfulness.'"

I am therefore in no way the first to presume that there is a sense and purpose behind the slight functional disturbances of the daily life of healthy people.[45]

If the lapse in speech, which is without doubt a motor function, admits of such a conception, it is quite natural to transfer to the lapses of our other motor functions the same expectation. I have here formed two groups of cases; all these cases in which the faulty effect seems to be the essential element—that is, the deviation from the intention—I denote as erroneously carried-out actions (*Vergreifen*); the others, in which the entire action appears rather inexpedient, I call "symptomatic and chance actions." But no distinct line of demarcation can be formed; indeed, we are forced to conclude that all divisions used in this treatise are of only descriptive significance and contradict the inner unity of the sphere of manifestation.

The psychologic understanding of erroneous actions apparently gains little in clearness when we place it under the head of "ataxia," and especially under "cortical ataxia." Let us rather try to trace the individual examples to their proper determinants. To do this I shall again resort to personal observations, the opportunities for which I could not very frequently find in myself.

(*a*) In former years, when I made more calls at the homes of patients than I do at present, it often happened, when I stood before a door where I should have knocked or rung the bell, that I would pull the key of my own house from my pocket, only to replace it, quite abashed. When I investigated in what patients' homes this occurred, I had to admit that the faulty action—taking out my key instead of ringing the bell—signified paying a certain tribute to the house where the error occurred. It was equivalent to the thought "Here I feel at home," as it happened only where I possessed the patient's regard. (Naturally, I never rang my own door-bell.) The faulty action was therefore a symbolic representation of a definite thought which was not accepted consciously as serious; for in reality the neurologist is well aware that the patient seeks him only so long as he expects to be benefited by him, and that his own excessively warm interest for his patient is evinced only as a means of psychic treatment. An almost identical repetition of my experience is described by A. Maeder ("Contrib. à la psychopathologie de la vie quotidienne," *Arch. de Psychol.*, vi., 1906): "Il est arrivé à chacun de sortir son trousseau, en arrivant à la porte d'un ami particulièrement cher, de se surprendre pour ainsi dire, en train d'ouvrir avec sa clé comme chez soi. C'est un retard, puisqu'il faut sonner malgré tout, mais c'est une preuve qu'on se sent—ou qu'on voudrait se sentir—comme chez soi, auprès de cet ami." Jones speaks as follows about the use of keys:[46] "The use of keys is a fertile source of occurrences of this kind, of which two examples may be given. If I am disturbed in the midst of some engrossing work at home by having to go to the hospital to carry out some routine work, I am very apt to find myself trying to open the door of my laboratory there with the key of my desk at home, although the two keys are quite unlike each other. The mistake unconsciously demonstrates where I would rather be at the moment.

"Some years ago I was acting in a subordinate position at a certain institution, the front door of which was kept locked, so that it was necessary to ring for admission. On several occasions I found myself making serious attempts to open the door with my house key. Each one of the permanent visiting staff, of which I aspired to be a member, was provided with a key to avoid the trouble of having to wait at the door. My mistake thus expressed the desire to be on a similar footing and to be quite 'at home' there." A similar experience is reported by Dr. Hans Sachs of Vienna: "I always carry two keys with me, one for the door of my office and one for my residence. They are not by any means easily interchanged, as the office key is at least three times as big as my house key. Besides, I carry the first in my trouser pocket and the other in my vest pocket. Yet it often happened that I noticed on reaching the door that while ascending the stairs I had taken out the wrong key. I decided to undertake a statistical examination; as I was daily in about the same emotional state when I stood before both doors, I thought that the interchanging of the two keys must show a regular tendency, if they were differently determined psychically. Observation of later occurrences showed that I regularly took out my house key before the office door. Only on one occasion was this reversed: I came home tired, knowing that I would find there a guest. I made an attempt to unlock the door with the, naturally too big, office key."

(*b*) At a certain time twice a day for six years I was accustomed to wait for admission before a door in the second story of the same house, and during this long period of time it happened twice (within a short interval) that I climbed a story higher. On the first of these occasions I was in an ambitious day-dream, which allowed me to "mount always higher and higher." In fact, at that time I heard the door in question open as I put my foot on the first step of the third flight. On the other occasion I again went too far "engrossed in thought." As soon as I became aware of it, I turned back and sought to snatch the dominating fantasy; I found that I was irritated over a criticism of my works, in which the reproach was made that I "always went too far," which I replaced by the less respectful expression "climbed too high."

(*c*) For many years a reflex hammer and a tuning-fork lay side by side on my desk. One day I hurried off at the close of my office hours, as I wished to catch a certain train, and, despite broad daylight, put the tuning-fork in my coat pocket in place of the reflex hammer. My attention was called to the mistake through the weight of the object drawing down my pocket. Any one unaccustomed to reflect on such slight occurrences would without hesitation explain the faulty action by the hurry of the moment, and excuse it. In spite of that, I preferred to ask myself why I took the tuning-fork instead of the hammer. The haste could just as well have been a motive for carrying out the action properly in order not to waste time over the correction. "Who last grasped the tuning-fork?" was the question which immediately flashed through my mind. It happened that only a few days ago an idiotic child, whose attention to sensory impressions I was testing, had been so fascinated by the tuning-fork that I found it difficult to tear it away from him. Could it mean, therefore, that I was an idiot? To be sure, so it would seem, as the next thought which associated itself with the hammer was *chamer* (Hebrew for "ass"). But what was the meaning of this abusive language? We must here inquire into the situation. I hurried to a consultation at a place on the Western railroad to see a patient who, according to the anamnesis which I received by letter, had fallen from a balcony some months before, and since then had been unable to walk. The physician who invited me wrote that he was still unable to say whether he was dealing with a spinal injury or traumatic neurosis—hysteria. That was what I was to decide. This could therefore be a reminder to be particularly careful in this delicate differential diagnosis. As it is, my colleagues think that hysteria is diagnosed far too carelessly where more serious matters are concerned. But the abuse is not yet justified. Yes, the next association was that the small railroad station is the same place in which, some years previous, I saw a young man who, after a certain emotional experience, could not walk properly. At that time I diagnosed his malady as hysteria, and later put him under psychic treatment; but it afterward turned out that my diagnosis was neither incorrect nor correct. A large number of the patient's symptoms were hysterical, and they promptly disappeared in the course of treatment. But back of these there was a visible remnant that could not be reached by therapy, and could be referred only to a multiple sclerosis. Those who saw the patient after me had no difficulty in recognizing the organic affection. I could scarcely have acted or judged differently, still the impression was that of a serious mistake; the promise of a cure which I had given him could naturally not be kept. The mistake in grasping the tuning-fork instead of the hammer could therefore be translated into the following words: "You fool, you ass, get yourself together this time, and be careful not to diagnose again a case of hysteria where there is an incurable disease, as you did in this place years ago in the case of the poor man!" And fortunately for this little analysis, even if unfortunately for my mood, this same man, now having a very spastic gait, had been to my office a few days before, one day after the examination of the idiotic child. We observe that this time it is the voice of self-criticism which makes itself perceptible through the mistake in grasping. The erroneously carried-out action is specially suited to express self-reproach. The present mistake attempts to represent the mistake which was committed elsewhere.

(*d*) It is quite obvious that grasping the wrong thing may also serve a whole series of other obscure purposes. Here is a first example: It is very seldom that I break anything. I am not particularly dexterous, but by virtue of the anatomic integrity of my nervous and muscular apparatus there are apparently no grounds in me for such awkward movements with undesirable results. I can recall no object in my home the counterpart of which I have ever broken. Owing to the narrowness of my study it has often been necessary for me to work in the most uncomfortable position among my numerous antique clay and stone objects, of which I have a small collection. So much is this true that onlookers have expressed fear lest I topple down something and shatter it. But it never happened. Then why did I brush to the floor the cover of my simple inkwell so that it broke into pieces? My inkstand is made of a flat piece of marble which is hollowed out for the reception of the glass inkwell; the inkwell has a marble cover with a knob of the same stone. A circle of bronze statuettes with small terra-cotta figures is set behind this inkstand. I seated myself at the desk to write, I made a remarkably awkward outward movement with the hand holding the pen-holder, and so swept the cover of the inkstand, which already lay on the desk, to the floor. It is not difficult to find the explanation. Some hours before my sister had been in the room to look at some of my new acquisitions. She found them very pretty, and then remarked: "Now the desk really looks very well, only the inkstand does not match. You must get a prettier one." I accompanied my sister out and did not return for several hours. But then, as it seems, I performed the execution of the condemned inkstand. Did I perhaps conclude from my sister's words that she intended to present me with a prettier inkstand on the next festive occasion, and did I shatter the unsightly old one in order to force her to carry out her signified intention? If that be so, then my swinging motion was only apparently awkward; in reality it was most skilful and designed, as it understood how to avoid all the valuable objects located near it. I actually believe that we must accept this explanation for a whole series of seemingly accidental awkward movements. It is true that on the surface these seem to show something violent and irregular, similar to spastic-ataxic movements, but on examination they seem to be dominated by some intention, and they accomplish their aim with a certainty that cannot be generally credited to conscious arbitrary motions. In both characteristics, the force as well as the sure aim, they show besides a resemblance to the motor manifestations of the hysterical neurosis, and in part also to the motor accomplishments of somnambulism, which here as well as there point to the same unfamiliar modification of the functions of innervation. In latter years, since I have been collecting such observations, it has happened several times that I have shattered and broken objects of some value, but the examination of these cases convinced me that it was never the result of accident or of my unintentional awkwardness. Thus, one morning while in my bath-robe and straw slippers I followed a sudden impulse as I passed a room, and hurled a slipper from my foot against the wall so that it brought down a beautiful little marble Venus from its bracket. As it fell to pieces I recited quite unmoved the following verse from Busch:—

"Ach! Die Venus ist perdü—[47]
Klickeradoms!—von Medici!"

This crazy action and my calmness at the sight of the damage is explained in the then existing situation. We had a very sick person in the family, of whose recovery I had personally despaired. That morning I had been informed that there was a great improvement; I know that I had said to myself, "After all she will live." My attack of destructive madness served therefore as the expression of a grateful feeling toward fate, and afforded me the opportunity of performing an "act of sacrifice," just as if I had vowed, "If she gets well I will give this or that as a sacrifice." That I chose the Venus of Medici as this sacrifice was only gallant homage to the convalescent. But even to-day it is still incomprehensible to me that I decided so quickly, aimed so accurately, and struck no other object in close proximity. Another breaking, in which I utilized a pen-holder falling from my hand, also signified a sacrifice, but this time it was a pious offering to avert some evil. I had once allowed myself to reproach a true and worthy friend for no other reason than certain manifestations which I interpreted from his unconscious activity. He took it amiss and wrote me a letter in which he bade me not to treat my friends by psychoanalysis. I had to admit that he was right and appeased him with my answer. While writing this letter I had before me my latest acquisition—a small, handsome glazed Egyptian figure. I broke it in the manner mentioned, and then immediately knew that I had caused this mischief to avert a greater one. Luckily, both the friendship and the figure could be so cemented that the break would not be noticed. A third case of breaking had a less serious connection; it was only a disguised "execution," to use an expression from Th. Vischer's *Auch Einer*, of an object that no longer suited my taste. For quite a while I had carried a cane with a silver handle; through no fault of mine the thin silver plate was once damaged and poorly repaired. Soon after the cane was returned I mirthfully used the handle to angle for the leg of one of my children. In that way it naturally broke, and I got rid of it. The indifference with which we accept the resulting damage in all these cases may certainly be taken as evidence for the existence of an unconscious purpose in their execution.

(*e*) As can sometimes be demonstrated by analysis, the dropping of objects or the overturning and breaking of the same are very frequently utilized as the expression of unconscious streams of thought, but more often they serve to represent the superstitious or odd significances connected therewith in popular sayings. The meanings attached to the spilling of salt, the overturning of a wineglass, the sticking of a knife dropped to the floor, and so on, are well known. I shall discuss later the right to investigate such superstitious interpretations; here I shall simply observe that the individual awkward acts do not by any means always have the same meaning, but, depending on the circumstances, they serve to represent now this or that purpose. Recently we passed through a period in my house during which an unusual number of glass and china dishes were broken. I myself largely contributed to this damage. This little endemic was readily explained by the fact that it preceded the public betrothal of my eldest daughter. On such festivities it is customary to break some dishes and utter at the same time some felicitating expression. This custom may signify a sacrifice or express any other symbolic sense. When servants destroy fragile objects through dropping them, we certainly do not think in the first place of a psychologic motive for it; still, some obscure motives are not improbable even here. Nothing lies farther from the uneducated than the appreciation of art and works of art. Our servants are dominated by a foolish hostility against these productions, especially when the objects, whose worth they do not realize, become a source of a great deal of work for them. On the other hand, persons of the same education and origin employed in scientific institutions often distinguish themselves by great dexterity and reliability in the handling of delicate objects, as soon as they begin to identify themselves with their masters and consider themselves an essential part of the staff. I shall here add the report of a young mechanical engineer, which gives some insight into the mechanism of damaging things. "Some time ago I worked with many others in the laboratory of the

High School on a series of complicated experiments on the subject of elasticity. It was a work that we undertook of our own volition, but it turned out that it took up more of our time than we expected. One day, while going to the laboratory with F., he complained of losing so much time, especially on this day, when he had so many other things to do at home. I could only agree with him, and he added half jokingly, alluding to an incident of the previous week: 'Let us hope that the machine will refuse to work, so that we can interrupt the experiment and go home earlier.' "In arranging the work, it happened that F. was assigned to the regulation of the pressure valve, that is, it was his duty to carefully open the valve and let the fluid under pressure flow from the accumulator into the cylinder of the hydraulic press. The leader of the experiment stood at the manometer and called a loud 'Stop!' when the maximum pressure was reached. At this command F. grasped the valve and turned it with all his force—to the left (all valves, without any exception, are closed to the right). This caused a sudden full pressure in the accumulator of the press, and as there was no outlet, the connecting pipe burst. This was quite a trifling accident to the machine, but enough to force us to stop our work for the day and go home.

"It is characteristic, moreover, that some time later, on discussing this occurrence, my friend F. could not recall the remark that I positively remember his having made."

Similarly, to fall, to make a misstep, or to slip need not always be interpreted as an entirely accidental miscarriage of a motor action. The linguistic double meaning of these expressions points to diverse hidden fantasies, which may present themselves through the giving up of bodily equilibrium. I recall a number of lighter nervous ailments in women and girls which made their appearance after falling without injury, and which were conceived as traumatic hysteria as a result of the shock of the fall. At that time I already entertained the impression that these conditions had a different connection, that the fall was already a preparation of the neurosis, and an expression of the same unconscious fantasies of sexual content which may be taken as the moving forces behind the symptoms. Was not this very thing meant in the proverb which says, "When a maiden falls, she falls on her back?" We can also add to these mistakes the case of one who gives a beggar a gold piece in place of a copper or a silver coin. The solution of such mishandling is simple: it is an act of sacrifice designed to mollify fate, to avert evil, and so on. If we hear a tender mother or aunt express concern regarding the health of a child, directly before taking a walk during which she displays her charity, contrary to her usual habit, we can no longer doubt the sense of this apparently undesirable accident. In this manner our faulty acts make possible the practice of all those pious and superstitious customs which must shun the light of consciousness, because of the strivings against them of our unbelieving reason.

(*f*) That accidental actions are really intentional will find no greater credence in any other sphere than in sexual activity, where the border between the intention and accident hardly seems discernible. That an apparently clumsy movement may be utilized in a most refined way for sexual purposes I can verify by a nice example from my own experience. In a friend's house I met a young girl visitor who excited in me a feeling of fondness which I had long believed extinct, thus putting me in a jovial, loquacious, and complaisant mood. At that time I endeavoured to find out how this came about, as a year before this same girl made no impression on me.

As the girl's uncle, a very old man, entered the room, we both jumped to our feet to bring him a chair which stood in the corner. She was more agile than I and also nearer the object, so that she was the first to take possession of the chair. She carried it with its back to her, holding both hands on the edge of the seat. As I got there later and did not give up the claim to carrying the chair, I suddenly stood directly back of her, and with both my arms was embracing her from behind, and for a moment my hands touched her lap. I naturally solved the situation as quickly as it came about. Nor did it occur to anybody how dexterously I had taken advantage of this awkward movement. Occasionally I have had to admit to myself that the annoying, awkward stepping aside on the street, whereby for some seconds one steps here and there, yet always in the same direction as the other person, until finally both stop facing each other, that this "barring one's way" repeats an ill-mannered, provoking conduct of earlier times and conceals erotic purposes under the mask of awkwardness. From my psychoanalysis of neurotics I know that the so-called naïveté of young people and children is frequently only such a mask, employed in order that the subject may say or do the indecent without restraint. W. Stekel has reported similar observations in regard to himself: "I entered a house and offered my right hand to the hostess. In a most remarkable way I thereby loosened the bow which held together her loose morning-gown. I was conscious of no dishonourable intent, still I executed this awkward movement with the agility of a juggler."

(*g*) The effects which result from mistakes of normal persons are, as a rule, of a most harmless nature. Just for this reason it would be particularly interesting to find out whether mistakes of considerable importance, which could be followed by serious results, as, for example, those of physicians or druggists, fall within the range of our point of view.

As I am seldom in a position to deal with active medical matters, I can only report one mistake from my own experience. I treated a very old woman, whom I visited twice daily for several years. My medical activities were limited to two acts, which I performed during my morning visits: I dropped a few drops of an eye lotion into her eyes and gave her a hypodermic injection of morphine. I prepared regularly two bottles—a blue one, containing the eye lotion, and a white one, containing the morphine solution. While performing these duties my thoughts were mostly occupied with something else, for they had been repeated so often that the attention acted as if free. One morning I noticed that the automaton worked wrong; I had put the dropper into the white instead of into the blue bottle, and had dropped into the eyes the morphine instead of the lotion. I was greatly frightened, but then calmed myself through the reflection that a few drops of a *two per cent.* solution of morphine would not likely do any harm even if left in the conjunctival sac. The cause of the fright manifestly belonged elsewhere.

In attempting to analyse the slight mistake I first thought of the phrase, "to seize the old woman by mistake," which pointed out the short way to the solution. I had been impressed by a dream which a young man had told me the previous evening, the contents of which could be explained only on the basis of sexual intercourse with his own mother.[48] The strangeness of the fact that the Œdipus legend takes no offence at the age of Queen Jocasta seemed to me to agree with the assumption that in being in love with one's mother we never deal with the present personality, but with her youthful memory picture carried over from our childhood. Such incongruities always show themselves where one fantasy fluctuating between two periods is made conscious, and is then bound to one definite period.

Deep in thoughts of this kind, I came to my patient of over ninety; I must have been well on the way to grasp the universal character of the Œdipus fable as the correlation of the fate which the oracle pronounces, for I made a blunder in reference to or on the old woman. Here, again, the mistake was harmless; of the two possible errors, taking the morphine solution for the eye, or the eye lotion for the injection, I chose the one by far the least harmful. The question still remains open whether in mistakes in handling things which may cause serious harm we can assume an unconscious intention as in the cases here discussed.

The following case from Brill's experience corroborates the assumption that even serious mistakes are determined by unconscious intentions: "A physician received a telegram informing him that his aged uncle was very sick. In spite of important family affairs at home he at once repaired to that distant town because his uncle was really his father, who had cared for him since he was one and a half years old, when his own father had died. On reaching there he found his uncle suffering from pneumonia, and, as the old man was an octogenarian, the doctors held out no hope for his recovery. 'It was simply a question of a day or two,' was the local doctor's verdict. Although a prominent physician in a big city, he refused to co-operate in the treatment, as he found that the case was properly managed by the local doctor, and he could not suggest anything to improve matters.

"Since death was daily expected, he decided to remain to the end. He waited a few days, but the sick man struggled hard, and although there was no question of any recovery, because of the many new complications which had arisen, death seemed to be deferred for a while. One night before retiring he went into the sick-room and took his uncle's pulse. As it was quite weak, he decided not to wait for the doctor, and administered a hypodermic injection. The patient grew rapidly worse and died within a few hours. There was something strange in the last symptoms, and on later attempting to replace the tube of hypodermic tablets into the case, he found to his consternation that he had taken out the wrong tube, and instead of a small dose of digitalis he had given a large dose of hyoscine.

"This case was related to me by the doctor after he read my paper on the Œdipus Complex.[49] We agreed that this mistake was determined not only by his impatience to get home to his sick child, but also by an old resentment and unconscious hostility toward his uncle (father)."

It is known that in the more serious cases of psychoneuroses one sometimes finds self-mutilations as symptoms of the disease. That the psychic conflict may end in suicide can never be excluded in these cases. Thus I know from experience, which some day I shall support with convincing examples, that many apparently accidental injuries happening to such patients are really self-inflicted. This is brought about by the fact that there is a constantly lurking tendency to self-punishment, usually expressing itself in self-reproach, or contributing to the formation of a symptom, which skilfully makes use of an external situation. The required external situation may accidentally present itself or the punishment tendency may assist it until the way is open for the desired injurious effect.

Such occurrences are by no means rare even in cases of moderate severity, and they betray the portion of unconscious intention through a series of special features—for example, through the striking presence of mind which the patients show in the pretended accidents.[50]

I will report exhaustively one in place of many such examples from my professional experience. A young woman broke her leg below the knee in a carriage accident so that she was bedridden for weeks. The striking part of it was the lack of any manifestation of pain and the calmness with which she bore her misfortune. This calamity ushered in a long and serious neurotic illness, from which she was finally cured by psychotherapy. During the treatment I discovered the circumstances surrounding the accident, as well as certain impressions which preceded it. The young woman with her jealous husband spent some time on the farm of her married sister, in company with her numerous other brothers and sisters with their wives and husbands. One evening she gave an exhibition of one of her talents before this intimate circle; she danced artistically the "cancan," to the great delight of her relatives, but to the great annoyance of her husband, who afterward whispered to her, "Again you have behaved like a prostitute." The words took effect; we will leave it undecided whether it was just on account of the dance. That night she was restless in her sleep, and the next forenoon she decided to go out driving. She chose the horses herself, refusing one team and demanding another. Her youngest sister wished to have her baby with its nurse accompany her, but she opposed this vehemently. During the drive she was nervous; she reminded the coachman that the horses were getting skittish, and as the fidgety animals really produced a momentary difficulty she jumped from the carriage in fright and broke her leg, while those remaining in the carriage were uninjured. Although after the disclosure of these details we can hardly doubt that this accident was really contrived, we cannot fail to admire the skill which forced the accident to mete out a punishment so suitable to the crime. For as it happened "cancan" dancing with her became impossible for a long time.

Concerning self-inflicted injuries of my own experience, I cannot report anything in calm times, but under extraordinary conditions I do not believe myself incapable of such acts. When a member of my family complains that he or she has bitten his tongue, bruised her finger, and so on, instead of the expected sympathy I put the question, "Why did you do that?" But I have most painfully squeezed my thumb, after a youthful patient acquainted me during the treatment with his intention (naturally not to be taken seriously) of marrying my eldest daughter, while I knew that she was then in a private hospital in extreme danger of losing her life.

One of my boys, whose vivacious temperament was wont to put difficulties in the management of nursing him in his illness, had a fit of anger one morning because he was ordered to remain in bed during the forenoon, and threatened to kill himself: a way out suggested to him by the newspapers. In the evening he showed me a swelling on the side of his chest which was the result of bumping against the door knob. To my ironical question why he did it, and what he meant by it, the eleven-year-old child explained, "That was my attempt at suicide which I threatened this morning." However, I do not believe that my views on self-inflicted wounds were accessible to my children at that time.

Whoever believes in the occurrence of semi-intentional self-inflicted injury—if this awkward expression be permitted—will become prepared to accept through it the fact that aside from conscious intentional suicide there also exists semi-intentional annihilation—with unconscious intention—which is capable of aptly utilizing a threat against life and masking it as a casual mishap. Such mechanism is by no means rare. For the tendency to self-destruction exists to a certain degree in many more persons than in those who bring it to completion. Self-inflicted injuries are, as a rule, a compromise between this impulse and the forces working against it, and even where it really comes to suicide the inclination has existed for a long time with less strength or as an unconscious and repressed tendency.

Even suicide consciously committed chooses its time, means, and opportunity; it is quite natural that unconscious suicide should wait for a motive to take upon itself one part of the causation and thus free it from its oppression by taking up the defensive forces of the person.[51] These are in no way idle discussions which I here bring up; more than one case of apparently accidental misfortune (on a horse or out of a carriage) has become known to me whose surrounding circumstances justified the suspicion of suicide.

For example, during an officers' horse-race one of the riders fell from his horse and was so seriously injured that a few days later he succumbed to his injuries. His behaviour after regaining consciousness was remarkable in more than one way, and his conduct previous to the accident was still more remarkable. He had been greatly depressed by the death of his beloved mother, had crying spells in the society of his comrades, and to his trusted friend had spoken of the *tædium vitæ*. He had wished to quit the service in order to take part in a war in Africa which had no interest for him.[52] Formerly a keen rider, he had later evaded riding whenever possible. Finally, before the horse-race, from which he could not withdraw, he expressed a sad foreboding, which most expectedly in the light of our conception came true. It may be contended that it is quite comprehensible without any further cause that a person in such a state of nervous depression cannot manage a horse as well as on normal days. I quite agree with that, only I should like to look for the mechanism of this motor inhibition through "nervousness" in the intention of self-destruction here emphasized.

Dr. Ferenczi has left to me for publication the analysis of an apparently accidental injury by shooting which he explained as an unconscious attempt at suicide. I can only agree with his deduction:—

"J. Ad., 22 years old, carpenter, visited me on the 18th of January, 1908. He wished to know whether the bullet which pierced his left temple March 20, 1907, could or should be removed by operation. Aside from occasional, not very severe, headaches, he felt quite well, also the objective examination showed nothing besides the characteristic powder wound on the left temple, so that I advised against an operation. When questioned concerning the circumstances of the case he asserted that he injured himself accidentally. He was playing with his brother's revolver, and *believing that it was not loaded* he pressed it with his left hand against the left temple (he is not left-handed), put his finger on the trigger, and the shot went off. *There were three bullets in the six-shooter.*

"I asked him how he came to carry the revolver, and he answered that it was at the time of his army conscription, that he took it to the inn the evening before because he feared fights. At the army examination he was considered unfit for service on account of varicose veins, which caused him much mortification. He went home and played with the revolver. He had no intention of hurting himself, but the accident occurred. On further questioning whether he was otherwise satisfied with his fortune, he answered with a sigh, and related a love affair with a girl who loved him in return, but nevertheless left him. She emigrated to America out of sheer avariciousness. He wanted to follow her, but his parents prevented him. His lady-love left on the 20th of January, 1907, just two months before the accident.

"Despite all these suspicious elements the patient insisted that the shot was an 'accident.' I was firmly convinced, however, that the neglect to find out whether the revolver was loaded before he began to play with it, as well as the self-inflicted injury, were psychically determined. He was still under the depressing effects of the unhappy love affair, and apparently wanted 'to forget everything' in the army. When this hope, too, was taken away from him he resorted to playing with the weapon—that is, to an unconscious attempt at suicide. The fact that he did not hold the revolver in the right but in the left hand speaks conclusively in favour of the fact that he was really only 'playing'—that is, he did not wish consciously to commit suicide."

Another analysis of an apparently accidental self-inflicted wound, detailed to me by an observer, recalls the saying, "He who digs a pit for others falls in himself."[53]

"Mrs. X., belonging to a good middle-class family, is married and has three children. She is somewhat nervous, but never needed any strenuous treatment, as she could sufficiently adapt herself to life. One day she sustained a rather striking though transitory disfigurement of her face in the following manner: She stumbled in a street that was in process of repair and struck her face against the house wall. The whole face was bruised, the eyelids blue and œdematous, and as she feared that something might happen to her eyes she sent for the doctor. After she was calmed I asked her, 'But why did you fall in such a manner?' She answered that just before this accident she warned her husband, who had been suffering for some months from a joint affection, to be very careful in the street, and she often had the experience that in some remarkable way those things occurred to her against which she warned others.

"I was not satisfied with this as the determination of her accident, and asked her whether she had not something else to tell me. 'Yes, just before the accident she noticed a nice picture in a shop on the other side of the street, which she suddenly desired as an ornament for her nursery, and wished to buy it at once. She thereupon walked across to the shop without looking at the street, stumbled over a heap of stones, and fell with her face against the wall without making the slightest effort to shield herself with her hands. The intention to buy the picture was immediately forgotten, and she walked home in haste.'

"'But why were you not more careful?' I asked.

"'Oh!' she answered, 'perhaps it was only a punishment for that episode which I confided to you!'

"'Has this episode still bothered you?'

"'Yes, later I regretted it very much; I considered myself wicked, criminal, and immoral, but at the time I was almost crazy with nervousness.'

"She referred to an abortion which was started by a quack and had to be brought to completion by a gynecologist. This abortion was initiated with the consent of her husband, as both wished, on account of their pecuniary circumstances, to be spared from being additionally blessed with children.

"She said: 'I had often reproached myself with the words, "You really had your child killed," and I feared that such a crime could not remain unpunished. Now that you have assured me that there is nothing seriously wrong with my eyes I am quite assured I have already been sufficiently punished.'

"This accident, therefore, was, on the one hand, a retribution for her sin, but, on the other hand, it may have served as an escape from a more dire punishment which she had feared for many months. In the moment that she ran to the shop to buy the picture the memory of this whole history, with its fears (already quite active in her unconscious at the time she warned her husband), became overwhelming and could perhaps find expression in words like these: 'But why do you want an ornament for the nursery?—you who had your child killed! You are a murderer! The great punishment is surely approaching!'

"This thought did not become conscious, but instead of it she made use of the situation—I might say of the psychologic moment—to utilize in a commonplace manner the heap of stones to inflict upon herself this punishment. It was for this reason that she did not even attempt to put out her arms while falling and was not much frightened. The second, and probably lesser, determinant of her accident was obviously the self-punishment for her unconscious wish to be rid of her husband, who was an accessory to the crime in this affair. This was betrayed by her absolutely superfluous warning to be very careful in the street on account of the stones. For, just because her husband had a weak leg, he was very careful in walking."

If such a rage against one's own integrity and one's own life can be hidden behind apparently accidental awkwardness and motor insufficiency, then it is not a big step forward to grasp the possibility of transferring the same conception to mistakes which seriously endanger the life and health of others. What I can put forward as evidence for the validity of this conception was taken from my experience with neurotics, and hence does not fully meet the demands of this situation. I will report a case in which it was not an erroneously carried-out action, but what may be more aptly termed a symbolic or chance action that gave me the clue which later made possible the solution of the patient's conflict.

I once undertook to improve the marriage relations of a very intelligent man, whose differences with his tenderly attached young wife could surely be traced to real causes, but as he himself admitted could not be altogether explained through them. He continually occupied himself with the thought of a separation, which he repeatedly rejected because he dearly loved his two small children. In spite of this he always returned to that resolution and sought no means to make the situation bearable to himself. Such an unsettlement of a conflict served to prove to me that there were unconscious and repressed motives which enforced the conflicting conscious thoughts, and in such cases I always undertake to end the conflict by psychic analysis. One day the man related to me a slight occurrence which had extremely frightened him. He was sporting with the older child, by far his favourite. He tossed it high in the air and repeated this tossing till finally he thrust it so high that its head almost struck the massive gas chandelier. Almost, but not quite, or say "just about!" Nothing happened to the child except that it became dizzy from fright. The father stood transfixed with the child in his arms, while the mother merged into an hysterical attack. The particular facility of this careless movement, with the violent reaction in the parents, suggested to me to look upon this accident as a symbolic action which gave expression to an evil intention toward the beloved child.

I could remove the contradiction of the actual tenderness of this father for his child by referring the impulse to injure it to the time when it was the only one, and so small that as yet the father had no occasion for tender interest in it. Then it was easy to assume that this man, so little pleased with his wife at that time, might have thought: "If this small being for whom I have no regard whatever should die, I would be free and could separate from my wife." The wish for the death of this much loved being must therefore have continued unconsciously. From here it was easy to find the way to the unconscious fixation of this wish.

There was indeed a powerful determinant in a memory from the patient's childhood: it referred to the death of a little brother, which the mother laid to his father's negligence, and which led to serious quarrels with threats of separation between the parents. The continued course of my patient's life, as well as the therapeutic success confirmed my analysis.

***

IX

SYMPTOMATIC AND CHANCE ACTIONS

The actions described so far, in which we recognize the execution of an unconscious intention, appeared as disturbances of other unintended actions, and hid themselves under the pretext of awkwardness. Chance actions, which we shall now discuss, differ from erroneously carried out actions only in that they disdain the support of a conscious intention and really need no pretext. They appear independently and are accepted because one does not credit them with any aim or purpose. We execute them "without thinking anything of them," "by mere chance," "just to keep the hands busy," and we feel confident that such information will be quite sufficient should one inquire as to their significance. In order to enjoy the advantage of this exceptional position these actions which no longer claim awkwardness as an excuse must fulfil certain conditions: they must not be striking, and their effects must be insignificant.

I have collected a large number of such "chance actions" from myself and others, and after thoroughly investigating the individual examples, I believe that the name "symptomatic actions" is more suitable. They give expression to something which the actor himself does not suspect in them, and which as a rule he has no intention of imparting to others, but aims to keep to himself. Like the other phenomena considered so far, they thus play the part of symptoms.

The richest output of such chance or symptomatic actions is above all obtained in the psychoanalytic treatment of neurotics. I cannot deny myself the pleasure of showing by two examples of this nature how far and how delicately the determination of these plain occurrences are swayed by unconscious thoughts. The line of demarcation between the symptomatic actions and the erroneously carried out actions is so indefinite that I could have disposed of these examples in the preceding chapter.

(*a*) During the analysis a young woman reproduced this idea which suddenly occurred to her. Yesterday while cutting her nails "she had cut into the flesh while engaged in trimming the cuticle." This is of so little interest that we ask in astonishment why it is at all remembered and mentioned, and therefore come to the conclusion that we deal with a symptomatic action. It was really the finger upon which the wedding-ring is worn which was injured through this slight awkwardness. It happened, moreover, on her wedding-day, which thus gives to the injury of the delicate skin a very definite and easily guessed meaning. At the same time she also related a dream which alluded to the awkwardness of her husband and her anesthesia as a woman. But why did she injure the ring finger of her left hand when the wedding-ring is worn on the right? Her husband is a jurist, a "Doctor of Laws" (*Doktor der Rechte*, literally a Doctor of Rights), and her secret affection as a girl belonged to a physician who was jokingly called *Doktor der Linke* (literally Doctor of Left). Incidentally a left-handed marriage has a definite meaning.

(*b*) A single young woman relates: "Yesterday, quite unintentionally, I tore a hundred-dollar note in two pieces and gave half to a woman who was visiting me. Is that, too, a symptomatic action?" After closer investigation the matter of the hundred-dollar note elicited the following associations: She dedicated a part of her time and her fortune to charitable work. Together with another woman she was taking care of the rearing of an orphan. The hundred dollars was the contribution sent her by that woman, which she enclosed in an envelope and provisionally deposited on her writing-desk.

The visitor was a prominent woman with whom she was associated in another act of charity. This woman wished to note the names of a number of persons to whom she could apply for charitable aid. There was no paper, so my patient grasped the envelope from her desk, and without thinking of its contents tore it in two pieces, one of which she kept, in order to have a duplicate list of names, and gave the other to her visitor.

Note the harmlessness of this aimless occurrence. It is known that a hundred-dollar note suffers no loss in value when it is torn, provided all the pieces are produced. That the woman would not throw away the piece of paper was assumed by the importance of the names on it, and there was just as little doubt that she would return the valuable content as soon as she noticed it.

But to what unconscious thought should this chance action, which was made possible through forgetfulness, give expression? The visitor in this case had a very definite relation to my patient and myself. It was she who at one time had recommended me as physician to the suffering girl, and if I am not mistaken my patient considered herself indebted for this advice. Should this halved hundred-dollar note perhaps represent a fee for her mediation? That still remained enigmatic.

But other material was added to this beginning. Several days before a woman mediator of a different sort had inquired of a relative whether the gracious young lady wished to make the acquaintance of a certain gentleman, and that morning, some hours before the woman's visit, the wooing letter of the suitor arrived, giving occasion for much mirth. When therefore the visitor opened the conversation with inquiries regarding the health of my patient, the latter could well have thought: "You certainly found me the right doctor, but if you could assist me in obtaining the right husband (and a child) I should be still more grateful."

Both mediators became fused into one in this repressed thought, and she handed the visitor the fee which her fantasy was ready to give the other. This resolution became perfectly convincing when I add that I had told her of such chance or symptomatic actions only the previous evening. She then took advantage of the next occasion to produce an analogous action.

We can undertake a grouping of these extremely frequent chance and symptomatic actions according to their occurrence as habitual, regular under certain circumstances, and as isolated ones. The first group (such as playing with the watch-chain, fingering one's beard, and so on), which can almost serve as a characteristic of the person concerned, is related to the numerous tic movements, and certainly deserves to be dealt with in connection with the latter. In the second group I place the playing with one's cane, the scribbling with one's pencil, the jingling of coins in one's pocket, kneading dough and other plastic materials, all sorts of handling of one's clothing, and many other actions of the same order.

These playful occupations during psychic treatment regularly conceal sense and meaning to which other expression is denied. Generally the person in question knows nothing about it; he is unaware whether he is doing the same thing or whether he has imitated certain modifications in his customary playing, and he also fails to see or hear the effects of these actions. For example, he does not hear the noise which is produced by the jingling of coins, and he is astonished and incredulous when his attention is called to it. Of equal significance to the physician, and worthy of his observation, is everything that one does with his clothing often without noticing it. Every change in the customary attire, every little negligence, such as an unfastened button, every trace of exposure means to express something that the wearer of the apparel does not wish to say directly, usually he is entirely unconscious of it.

The interpretation of these trifling chance actions, as well as the proof for their interpretation, can be demonstrated every time with sufficient certainty from the surrounding circumstances during the treatment, from the themes under discussion, and from the ideas that come to the surface when attention is directed to the seeming accident. Because of this connection I will refrain from supporting my assertions by reporting examples with their analyses; but I mention these matters because I believe that they have the same meaning in normal persons as in my patients.

I cannot, however, refrain from showing by at least one example how closely an habitually accomplished symbolic action may be connected with the most intimate and important part of the life of a normal individual.[54]

"As Professor Freud has taught us, the symbolism in the infantile life of the normal plays a greater rôle than was expected from earlier psychoanalytic experiences. In view of this the following brief analysis may be of general interest, especially on account of its medical aspects.

"A doctor on rearranging his furniture in a new house came across a straight, wooden stethoscope, and, after pausing to decide where he should put it, was impelled to place it on the side of his writing-desk in such a position that it stood exactly between his chair and the one reserved for his patients. The act in itself was certainly odd, for in the first place the straight stethoscope served no purpose, as he invariably used a binaural one; and in the second place all his medical apparatus and instruments were always kept in drawers, with the sole exception of this one. However, he gave no thought to the matter until one day it was brought to his notice by a patient who had never seen a wooden stethoscope, asking him what it was. On being told, she asked why he kept it there. He answered in an offhand way that that place was as good as any other. This, however, started him thinking, and he wondered whether there had been an unconscious motive in his action. Being interested in the psychoanalytic method, he asked me to investigate the matter.

"The first memory that occurred to him was the fact that when a medical student he had been struck by the habit his hospital interne had of always carrying in his hand a wooden stethoscope on his ward visits, although he never used it. He greatly admired this interne, and was much attached to him. Later on, when he himself became an interne he contracted the same habit, and would feel very uncomfortable if by mistake he left the room without having the instrument to swing in his hand. The aimlessness of the habit was shown, not only by the fact that the only stethoscope he ever used was a binaural one, which he carried in his pocket, but also in that it was continued when he was a surgical interne and never needed any stethoscope at all.

"From this it was evident that the idea of the instrument in question had in some way or other become invested with a greater psychic significance than normally belongs to it—in other words, that to the subject it stood for more than it does for other people. The idea must have got unconsciously associated with some other one, which it symbolized, and from which it derived its additional fulness of meaning. I will forestall the rest of the analysis by saying what this secondary idea was—namely, a phallic one; the way in which this curious association had been formed will presently be related. The discomfort he experienced in hospital on missing the instrument, and the relief and assurance the presence of it gave him, was related to what is known as a 'castration-complex'—namely, a childhood fear, often continued in a disguised form into adult life, lest a private part of his body should be taken away from him, just as playthings so often were. The fear was due to paternal threats that it would be cut off if he were not a good boy, particularly in a certain direction. This is a very common complex, and accounts for a great deal of general nervousness and lack of confidence in later years.

"Then came a number of childhood memories relating to his family doctor. He had been strongly attached to this doctor as a child, and during the analysis long-buried memories were recovered of a double phantasy he had in his fourth year concerning the birth of a younger sister—namely, that she was the child (1) of himself and his mother, the father being relegated to the background, and (2) of the doctor and himself; in this he thus played both a masculine and feminine part.[55] At the time, when his curiosity was being aroused by the event, he could not help noticing the prominent share taken by the doctor in the proceedings, and the subordinate position occupied by the father: the significance of this for his later life will presently be pointed out.

"The stethoscope association was formed through many connections. In the first place, the physical appearance of the instrument—a straight, rigid, hollow tube, having a small bulbous summit at one extremity and a broad base at the other—and the fact of its being the essential part of the medical paraphernalia, the instrument with which the doctor performed his magical and interesting feats, were matters that attracted his boyish attention. He had had his chest repeatedly examined by the doctor at the age of six, and distinctly recollected the voluptuous sensation of feeling the latter's head near him pressing the wooden stethoscope into his chest, and of the rhythmic to-and-fro respiratory movement. He had been struck by the doctor's habit of carrying his stethoscope inside his hat; he found it interesting that the doctor should carry his chief instrument concealed about his person, always handy when he went to see patients, and that he only had to take off his hat (*i.e.*, a part of his clothing) and 'pull it out.' At the age of eight he was impressed by being told by an older boy that it was the doctor's custom to get into bed with his women patients. It is certain that the doctor, who was young and handsome, was extremely popular among the women of the neighbourhood, including the subject's own mother. The doctor and his 'instrument' were therefore the objects of great interest throughout his boyhood.

"It is probable that, as in many other cases, unconscious identification with the family doctor had been a main motive in determining the subject's choice of profession. It was here doubly conditioned (1) by the superiority of the doctor on certain interesting occasions to the father, of whom the subject was very jealous, and (2) by the doctor's knowledge of forbidden topics[56] and his opportunity for illicit indulgence. The subject admitted that he had on several occasions experienced erotic temptations in regard to his women patients; he had twice fallen in love with one, and finally had married one.

"The next memory was of a dream, plainly of a homosexual-masochistic nature; in it a man, who proved to be a replacement figure of the family doctor, attacked the subject with a 'sword.' The idea of a sword, as is so frequently the case in dreams, represented the same idea that was mentioned above to be associated with that of a wooden stethoscope. The thought of a sword reminded the subject of the passage in the *Nibelung Saga*, where Sigurd sleeps with his naked sword

(*Gram*) between him and Brunhilda, an incident that had always greatly struck his imagination.

"The meaning of the symptomatic act now at last became clear. The subject had placed his wooden stethoscope between him and his patients, just as Sigurd had placed his sword (an equivalent symbol) between him and the maiden he was not to touch. The act was a compromise-formation; it served both to gratify in his imagination the repressed wish to enter into nearer relations with an attractive patient (interposition of phallus), and at the same time to remind him that this wish was not to become a reality (interposition of sword). It was, so to speak, a charm against yielding to temptation.

"I might add that the following passage from Lord Lytton's *Richelieu* made a great impression on the boy:—

'Beneath the rule of men entirely great
The pen is mightier than the sword,'[57]

and that he became a prolific writer and uses an unusually large fountain-pen. When I asked him what need he had of this pen, he replied in a characteristic manner, 'I have so much to express.'

"This analysis again reminds us of the profound views that are afforded us in the psychic life through the 'harmless' and 'senseless' actions, and how early in life the tendency to symbolization develops."

I can also relate an experience from my psychotherapeutic practice in which the hand, playing with a mass of bread-crumbs, gave evidence of an eloquent declaration. My patient was a boy not yet thirteen years of age, who had been very hysterical for two years. I finally took him for psychoanalytic treatment, after a lengthy stay at a hydrotherapeutic institution had proved futile. My supposition was that he must have had sexual experiences, and that, corresponding to his age, he had been troubled by sexual questions; but I was cautious about helping him with explanations as I wished to test further my assumption. I was therefore curious as to the manner in which the desired material would evince itself in him.

One day it struck me that he was rolling something between the fingers of his right hand; he would thrust it into his pocket and there continue playing with it, then would draw it out again, and so on. I did not ask what he had in his hand; but as he suddenly opened his hand he showed it to me. It was bread-crumbs kneaded into a mass. At the next session he again brought along a mass, and in the course of our conversation, although his eyes were closed, modelled a figure with an incredible rapidity which excited my interest. Without doubt it was a manikin like the crudest prehistoric idols, with a head, two arms, two legs, and an appendage between the legs which he drew out to a long point.

This was scarcely completed when he kneaded the manikin together again: later he allowed it to remain, but modelled an identical appendage on the flat of the back and on other parts in order to veil the meaning of the first. I wished to show him that I had understood him, but at the same time I wanted to deprive him of the evasion that he had thought of nothing while actively forming these figures. With this intention I suddenly asked him whether he remembered the story of the Roman king who gave his son's envoy a pantomimic answer in his garden.

The boy did not wish to recall what he must have learned so much more recently than I. He asked if that was the story of the slave on whose bald skull the answer was written. I told him, "No, that belonged to Greek history," and related the following: "King Tarquinius Superbus had induced his son Sextus to steal into a Latin city. The son, who had later obtained a foothold in the city, sent a messenger to the king asking what steps he should take next. The king gave no answer, but went into his garden, had the question repeated there, and silently struck off the heads of the largest and most beautiful poppies. All that the messenger could do was to report this to Sextus, who understood his father, and caused the most distinguished citizens of the city to be removed by assassination."

While I was speaking the boy stopped kneading, and as I was relating what the king did in his garden, I noticed that at the words "silently struck" he tore off the head of the manikin with a movement as quick as lightning. He therefore understood me, and showed that he was also understood by me. Now I could question him directly, and gave him the information that he desired, and in a short time the neurosis came to an end.

The symptomatic actions which we observe in inexhaustible abundance in healthy as well as in nervous people are worthy of our interest for more than one reason. To the physician they often serve as valuable indications for orienting himself in new or unfamiliar conditions; to the keen observer they often betray everything, occasionally even more than he cares to know. He who is familiar with its application sometimes feels like King Solomon, who, according to the Oriental legend, understood the language of animals.

One day I was to examine a strange young man at his mother's home. As he came towards me I was attracted by a large stain on his trousers, which by its peculiar stiff edges I recognized as one produced by albumen. After a moment's embarrassment the young man excused this stain by remarking that he was hoarse and therefore drank a raw egg, and that some of the slippery white of the egg had probably fallen on his clothes. To confirm his statements he showed the eggshell which could still be seen on a small plate in the room. The suspicious spot was thus explained in this harmless way; but as his mother left us alone I thanked him for having so greatly facilitated the diagnosis for me, and without further procedure I took as the topic of our discussion his confession that he was suffering from the effects of masturbation.

Another time I called on a woman as rich as she was miserly and foolish, who was in the habit of giving the physician the task of working his way through a heap of her complaints before he could reach the simple cause of her condition. As I entered she was sitting at a small table engaged in arranging silver dollars in little piles: as she rose she tumbled some of the pieces of money to the floor. I helped her pick them up, but interrupted the recitation of her misery by remarking: "Has your good son-in-law been spending so much of your money again?" She bitterly denied this, only to relate a few moments later the lamentable story of the aggravation caused by her son-in-law's extravagances. And she has not sent for me since. I cannot maintain that one always makes friends of those to whom he tells the meaning of their symptomatic actions.

He who observes his fellow-men while at table will be able to verify in them the nicest and most instructive symptomatic actions.

Dr. Hans Sachs relates the following:—

"I happened to be present when an elderly couple related to me partook of their supper. The lady had stomach trouble and was forced to follow a strict diet. A roast was put before the husband, and he requested his wife, who was not allowed to partake of this food, to give him the mustard. The wife opened the closet and took out the small bottle of stomach drops, and placed it on the table before her husband. Between the barrel-shaped mustard-glass and the small drop-bottle there was naturally no similarity through which the mishandling could be explained; yet the wife only noticed the mistake after her husband laughingly called her attention to it. The sense of this symptomatic action needs no explanation."

For an excellent example of this kind which was very skilfully utilized by the observer, I am indebted to Dr. Bernh. Dattner (Vienna):—

"I dined in a restaurant with my colleague H., a doctor of philosophy. He spoke about the injustice done to probationary students, and added that even before he finished his studies he was placed as secretary to the ambassador, or rather the extraordinary plenipotentiary Minister to Chili. 'But,' he added, 'the minister was afterwards transferred, and I did not make any effort to meet the newly appointed.' While uttering the last sentence he was lifting a piece of pie to his mouth, but he let it drop as if out of awkwardness. I immediately grasped the hidden sense of this symptomatic action, and remarked to my colleague, who was unacquainted with psychoanalysis, 'You really allowed a very choice morsel to slip from you.' He did not realize, however, that my words could equally refer to his symptomatic action, and he repeated the same words I uttered with a peculiarly agreeable and surprising vividness, as if I had actually taken the words from his mouth: 'It was really a very choice morsel that I allowed to get away from me.' He then followed this remark with a detailed description of his clumsiness, which has cost him this very remunerative position.

"The sense of this symbolic action becomes clearer if we remember that my colleague had scruples about telling me, almost a perfect stranger, concerning his precarious material situation, and his repressed thought took on the mask of symptomatic action which expressed symbolically what was meant to be concealed, and the speaker thus got relief from his unconscious."

That the taking away or taking along things without any apparent intention may prove to be senseful may be shown by the following examples.

I. Dr. B. Dattner relates: "An acquaintance paid the first after-marriage visit to a highly regarded lady friend of his youth. He told me of this visit and expressed his surprise at the fact that he failed in his resolution to visit with her only a short time, and then reported to me a rather strange faulty act which happened to him there.

"The husband of this friend, who took part in the conversation, was looking for a box of matches which he was sure was on the table when he came there. My acquaintance, too, looked through his pockets to ascertain whether he had not put it in his pocket, but without avail. Some time later he actually found it in his pocket, and was struck by the fact that there was only one match in the box.

"A dream a few days later showing the box symbolism in reference to the friend of his youth confirmed my explanation. With the symptomatic action my acquaintance meant to announce his priority-right and the exclusiveness of his possession (it contained only one match)."

Dr. Hans Sachs relates the following: "Our cook is very fond of a certain kind of pie. There is no possible doubt about this, as it is the only kind of pastry which she always prepares well. One Sunday she brought this pie to the table, took it off the pie-plate, and proceeded to remove the dishes used in the former course, but on the top of this pile she placed the pie, and disappeared with it into the kitchen. We first thought that she had something to improve on the pie, but as she failed to appear my wife rang the bell and asked, 'Betty, what happened to the pie?' to which the girl answered, without comprehending the question, 'How is that?' We had to call her attention to the fact that she carried the pie back to the kitchen. She had put it on the pile of dishes, taken it out, and put it away 'without noticing it.'

"The next day, when we were about to consume the rest of the pie, my wife noticed that there was as much of it as we had left the day before—that is, the girl had disdained to eat the portion of her favourite dish which was rightly hers. Questioned why she did not eat the pie, she answered, somewhat embarrassed, that she did not care for it.

"The infantile attitude is distinctly noticeable on both occasions—first the childish insatiableness in refusing to share with anybody the object of her wishes, then the reaction of spite which is just as childish: 'If you grudge it to me, keep it for yourself, I want nothing of it.'"

Chance or symptomatic actions occurring in affairs of married life have often a most serious significance, and could lead those who do not concern themselves with the psychology of the unconscious to a belief in omens. It is not an auspicious beginning if a young woman loses her wedding-ring on her wedding-tour, even if it were only mislaid and soon found.

I know a woman, now divorced, who in the management of her business affairs frequently signed her maiden name many years before she actually resumed it.

Once I was the guest of a newly married couple and heard the young woman laughingly relate her latest experience, how, on the day succeeding her return from the wedding tour she had sought out her single sister in order to go shopping with her as in former times, while her husband was attending business. Suddenly she noticed a man on the opposite side of the street; nudging her sister she said, "Why, that is surely Mr. L." She forgot that for some weeks this man had been her husband. I was chilled at this tale, but I did not dare draw any inferences. The little story came back to me only several years later, after this marriage had ended most unhappily.

The following observation, which could as well have found a place among the examples of forgetting, was taken from a noteworthy work published in French by A. Maeder.[58]

"Une dame nous racontait récement qu'elle avait oublie d'essayer sa robe de noce et s'en souvint la veille du marriage, à huit heur du soir, la couturière désespérait de voir sa cliente. Ce détail suffit à montrer que la fiancée ne se sentait pas très heureuse de porter une robe d'épouse, elle cherchait à oublier cette représentation pénible. Elle est aujourd'hui ... divorcée."

A friend who has learned to observe signs related to me that the great actress Eleanora Duse introduces a symptomatic action into one of her rôles which shows very nicely from what depth she draws her acting. It is a drama dealing with adultery; she has just been discussing with her husband and now stands soliloquizing before the seducer makes his appearance. During this short interval she plays with her wedding-ring, she pulls it off, replaces it, and finally takes it off again. She is now ready for the other.

I know of an elderly man who married a young girl, and instead of starting at once on his wedding tour he decided to spend the night in a hotel. Scarcely had they reached the hotel, when he noticed with fright that he was without his wallet, in which he had the entire sum of money for the wedding tour; he must have mislaid or lost it. He was still able to reach his servant by telephone; the latter found the missing article in the coat discarded for the travelling clothes and brought it to the hotel to the waiting bridegroom, who had thus entered upon his marriage without means.

It is consoling to think that the "losing of objects" by people is merely an unsuspected extension of a symptomatic action, and is thus welcome at least to the secret intention of the loser. Often it is only an expression of slight appreciation of the lost article, a secret dislike for the same, or perhaps for the person from whom it came, or the desire to lose this object was transferred to it from other and more important objects through symbolic association. The loss of valuable articles serves as an expression of diverse feelings; it may either symbolically represent a repressed thought—that is, it may bring back a memory which one would rather not hear—or it may represent a sacrifice to the obscure forces of fate, the worship of which is not yet entirely extinct even with us.[59]

The following examples will illustrate these statements concerning the losing of objects:—

Dr. B. Dattner states: "A colleague related to me that he lost his steel pencil which he had had for over two years, and which, on account of its superior quality, was highly prized by him. Analysis elicited the following facts: The day before he had received a very disagreeable letter from his brother-in-law, the concluding sentence of which read: 'At present I have neither the desire nor the time to assist you in your carelessness and laziness.' The effect connected with this letter was so powerful that the next day he promptly sacrificed the pencil which was a present from this brother-in-law in order not to be burdened with his favours."

Brill reports the following example: "A doctor took exception to the following statement in my book, 'We never lose what we really want' (*Psychanalysis, its Theories and Practical Application*, p. 214). His wife, who is very interested in psychologic subjects, read with him the chapter on "Psychopathology of Everyday Life"; they were both very much impressed with the novelty of the ideas, and so on, and were very willing to accept most of the statements. He could not, however, agree with the above-given statement because, as he said to his wife, 'I surely did not wish to lose my knife.' He referred to a valuable knife given to him by his wife, which he highly prized, the loss of which caused him much pain.

"It did not take his wife very long to discover the solution for this loss in a manner to convince them both of the accuracy of my statement. When she presented him with this knife he was a bit loath to accept it. Although he considered himself quite emancipated, he nevertheless entertained some superstition about giving or accepting a knife as a gift, because it is said that a knife cuts friendship. He even remarked this to his wife, who only laughed at his superstition. He had the knife for years before it disappeared.

"Analysis brought out the fact that the disappearance of the knife was directly connected with a period when there were violent quarrels between himself and his wife, which threatened to end in separation. They lived happily together until his step-daughter (it was his second marriage) came to live with them. His daughter was the cause of many misunderstandings, and it was at the height of these quarrels that he lost the knife.

"The unconscious activity is very nicely shown in this symptomatic action. In spite of his apparent freedom from superstition, he still unconsciously believed that a donated knife may cut friendship between the persons concerned. The losing of it was simply an unconscious defence against losing his wife, and by sacrificing the knife he made the superstitious ban impotent."

In a lengthy discussion and with the aid of dream analysis[60] Otto Rank made clear the sacrificial tendency with its deep-reaching motivation. It must be said that just such symptomatic actions often give us access to the understanding of the intimate psychic life of the person.

Of the many isolated chance-actions, I will relate one example which showed a deeper meaning even without analysis. This example clearly explains the conditions under which such symptoms may be produced most casually, and also shows that an observation of practical importance may be attached to it. During a summer tour it happened that I had to wait several days at a certain place for the arrival of my travelling companions. In the meantime I made the acquaintance of a young man, who also seemed lonely and was quite willing to join me. As we lived at the same hotel it was quite natural that we should take all our meals and our walks together.

On the afternoon of the third day he suddenly informed me that he expected his wife to arrive on that evening's express train. My psychologic interest was now aroused, as it had already struck me that morning that my companion rejected my proposal to make a long excursion, and in our short walk he objected to a certain path as too steep and dangerous. During our afternoon walk he suddenly thought that I must be hungry and insisted that I should not delay my evening meal on his account, that he would not sup before his wife's arrival. I understood the hint and seated myself at the table while he went to the station.

The next morning we met in the foyer of the hotel. He presented me to his wife, and added, "Of course, you will breakfast with us?" I had to attend first to a small matter in the next street, but assured him that I would return shortly. Later, as I entered the breakfast-room, I noticed that the couple were at a small table near the window, both seated on the same side of it. On the opposite side there was only one chair, which was covered, however, with a man's large and heavy coat. I understood well the meaning of this unintentional, none the less expressive, disposition of the coat. It meant this: "There is no room for you here, you are superfluous now."

The man did not notice that I remained standing before the table, being unable to take the seat, but his wife noticed it, and quickly nudged her husband and whispered: "Why, you have covered the gentleman's place with your coat."

These as well as other similar experiences have caused me to think that the actions executed unintentionally must inevitably become the source of misunderstanding in human relations. The perpetrator of the act, who is unaware of any associated intention, takes no account of it, and does not hold himself responsible for it. On the other hand, the second party, having regularly utilized even such acts as those of his partner to draw conclusions as to their purpose and meaning, recognizes more of the stranger's psychic processes than the latter is ready either to admit or believe that he has imparted. He becomes indignant when these conclusions drawn from his symptomatic actions are held up to him; he declares them baseless because he does not see any conscious intention in their execution, and complains of being misunderstood by the other. Close examination shows that such misunderstandings are based on the fact that the person is too fine an observer and understands too much. The more "nervous" two persons are the more readily will they give each other cause for disputes, which are based on the fact that one as definitely denies about his own person what he is sure to accept about the other.

And this is, indeed, the punishment for the inner dishonesty to which people grant expression under the guise of "forgetting," of erroneous actions and accidental emotions, a feeling which they would do better to confess to themselves and others when they can no longer control it. As a matter of fact it can be generally affirmed that every one is continually practising psychoanalysis on his neighbours, and consequently learns to know them better than each individual knows himself. The road following the admonition γν?θι σεα?τ?ν leads through the study of one's own apparently casual commissions and omissions.

***

X

ERRORS

Errors of memory are distinguished from forgetting and false recollections through one feature only, namely, that the error (false recollection) is not recognized as such but finds credence. However, the use of the expression "error" seems to depend on still another condition. We speak of "erring" instead of "falsely recollecting" where the character of the objective reality is emphasized in the psychic material to be reproduced—that is, where something other than a fact of my own psychic life is to be remembered, or rather something that may be confirmed or refuted through the memory of others. The reverse of the error in memory in this sense is formed by ignorance.

In my book *The Interpretation of Dreams*,[61] I was responsible for a series of errors in historical, and above all, in material facts, which I was astonished to discover after the appearance of the book. On closer examination I found that they did not originate from my ignorance, but could be traced to errors of memory explainable by means of analysis.

(*a*) On page 361 I indicated as *Schiller's* birthplace the city of *Marburg*, a name which recurs in *Styria*. The error is found in the analysis of a dream during a night journey from which I was awakened by the conductor calling out the name of the station *Marburg*. In the contents of the dream inquiry is made concerning a book by *Schiller*. But *Schiller* was not born in the university town of *Marburg* but in the Swabian city *Marbach*. I maintain that I always knew this.

(*b*) On page 165 *Hannibal's* father is called *Hasdrubal*. This error was particularly annoying to me, but it was most corroborative of my conception of such errors. Few readers of the book are better posted on the history of the *Barkides* than the author who wrote this error and overlooked it in three proofs. The name of Hannibal's father was *Hamilcar Barkas*; *Hasdrubal* was the name of *Hannibal's* brother as well as that of his brother-in-law and predecessor in command.

(*c*) On pages 217 and 492 I assert that *Zeus* emasculates his father *Kronos*, and hurls him from the throne. This horror I have erroneously advanced by a generation; according to Greek mythology it was *Kronos* who committed this on his father *Uranos*.[62]

How is it to be explained that my memory furnished me with false material on these points, while it usually places the most remote and unusual material at my disposal, as the readers of my books can verify? And, what is more, in three carefully executed proof-readings I passed over these errors as if struck blind.

Goethe said of Lichtenberg: "Where he cracks a joke, there lies a concealed problem." Similarly we can affirm of these passages cited from my book: back of every error is a repression. More accurately stated: the error conceals a falsehood, a disfigurement which is ultimately based on repressed material. In the analysis of the dreams there reported, I was compelled by the very nature of the theme to which the dream thoughts related, on the one hand, to break off the analysis in some places before it had reached its completion, and on the other hand, to remove an indiscreet detail through a slight disfigurement of its outline. I could not act differently, and had no other choice if I was at all to offer examples and illustrations. My constrained position was necessarily brought about by the peculiarity of dreams, which give expression to repressed thoughts, or to material which is incapable of becoming conscious. In spite of this it is said that enough material remained to offend the more sensitive souls. The disfigurement or concealment of the continuing thoughts known to me could not be accomplished without leaving some trace. What I wished to repress has often against my will obtruded itself on what I have taken up, and evinced itself in the matter as an unnoticeable error. Indeed, each of the three examples given is based on the same theme: the errors are the results of repressed thoughts which occupy themselves with my deceased father.

(*ad a*) Whoever reads through the dream analysed on page 361 will find some parts unveiled; in some parts he will be able to divine through allusions that I have broken off the thoughts which would have contained an unfavourable criticism of my father. In the continuation of this line of thoughts and memories there lies an annoying tale, in which books and a business friend of my father, named *Marburg*, play a part; it is the same name the calling out of which in the southern railway-station had aroused me from sleep. I wished to suppress this Mr. *Marburg* in the analysis from myself and my readers: he avenged himself by intruding where he did not belong, and changed the name of Schiller's birthplace from *Marbach* to *Marburg*.

(*ad b*) The error *Hasdrubal* in place of *Hamilcar*, the name of the brother instead of that of the father, originated from an association which dealt with the Hannibal fantasies of my college years and my dissatisfaction with the conduct of my father towards the "enemies of our people." I could have continued and recounted how my attitude toward my father was changed by a visit to England, where I made the acquaintance of my half-brother, by a previous marriage of my father. My brother's oldest son was my age exactly. Thus the age relations were no hindrance to a fantasy which may be stated thus: how much pleasanter it would be had I been born the son of my brother instead of the son of my father! This suppressed fantasy then falsified the text of my book at the point where I broke off the analysis, by forcing me to put the name of the brother for that of the father.

(*ad c*) The influence of the memory of this same brother is responsible for my having advanced by a generation the mythological horror of the Greek deities. One of the admonitions of my brother has lingered long in my memory. "Do not forget one thing concerning your conduct in life," he said: "you belong not to the second but really to the third generation of your father." Our father had remarried at an advanced age, and was therefore an old man to his children by the second marriage. I commit the error mentioned where I discuss the piety between parents and children.

Several times friends and patients have called my attention to the fact that in reporting their dreams or alluding to them in dream analyses, I have related inaccurately the circumstances experienced by us in common. These are also historic errors. On re-examining such individual cases I have found that my recollection of the facts was unreliable only where I had purposely disfigured or concealed something in the analysis. Here again we have *an unobserved error as a substitute for an intentional concealment or repression.*

From these errors, which originate from repression, we must sharply distinguish those which are based on actual ignorance. Thus, for example, it was ignorance when on my excursion to Wachau I believed that I had passed the resting-place of the revolutionary leader Fischof. Only the name is common to both places. *Fischof's Emmersdorf* is located in Kärnthen. But I did not know any better.

Here is another embarrassing but instructive error, an example of temporary ignorance if you like. One day a patient reminded me to give him the two books on Venice which I had promised him, as he wished to use them in planning his Easter tour. I answered that I had them ready and went into the library to fetch them, though the truth of the matter was that I had forgotten to look them up, since I did not quite approve of my patient's journey, looking upon it as an unnecessary interruption to the treatment, and as a material loss to the physician. Thereupon I made a quick survey of the library for the books.

One was *Venedig als Kunststätte*, and besides this I imagined I had an historic work of a similar order. Certainly there was *Die Mediceer (The Medicis)*; I took them and brought them in to him, then, embarrassed, I confessed my error. Of course I really knew that the Medicis had nothing to do with Venice, but for a short time it did not appear to me at all incorrect. Now I was compelled to practise justice; as I had so frequently interpreted my patient's symptomatic actions I could save my prestige only by being honest and admitting to him the secret motives of my averseness to his trip.

It may cause general astonishment to learn how much stronger is the impulse to tell the truth than is usually supposed. Perhaps it is a result of my occupation with psychoanalysis that I can scarcely lie any more. As often as I attempt a distortion I succumb to an error or some other faulty act, which betrays my dishonesty, as was manifest in this and in the preceding examples.

Of all faulty actions the mechanism of the error seems to be the most superficial. That is, the occurrence of the error invariably indicates that the mental activity concerned had to struggle with some disturbing influence, although the nature of the error need not be determined by the quality of the disturbing idea, which may have remained obscure. It is not out of place to add that the same state of affairs may be assumed in many simple cases of lapses in speaking and writing. Every time we commit a lapse in speaking or writing we may conclude that through mental processes there has come a disturbance which is beyond our intention. It may be conceded, however, that lapses in speaking and writing often follow the laws of similarity and convenience, or the tendency to acceleration, without allowing the disturbing element to leave a trace of its own character in the error resulting from the lapses in speaking or writing. It is the responsiveness of the linguistic material which at first makes possible the determination of the error, but it also limits the same.

In order not to confine myself exclusively to personal errors I will relate a few examples which could just as well have been ranged under "Lapses in Speech" or under "Erroneously Carried-out Actions," but as all these forms of faulty action have the same value they may as well be reported here.

(*a*) I forbade a patient to speak on the telephone to his lady-love, with whom he himself was willing to break off all relations, as each conversation only renewed the struggling against it. He was to write her his final decision, although there were some difficulties in the way of delivering the letter to her. He visited me at one o'clock to tell me that he had found a way of avoiding these difficulties, and among other things he asked me whether he might refer to me in my professional capacity.

At two o'clock while he was engaged in composing the letter of refusal, he interrupted himself suddenly, and said to his mother, "Well, I have forgotten to ask the Professor whether I may use his name in the letter." He hurried to the telephone, got the connection, and asked the question, "May I speak to the Professor after his dinner?" In answer he got an astonished "Adolf, have you gone crazy!" The answering voice was the very voice which at my command he had listened to for the last time. He had simply "made a mistake," and in place of the physician's number had called up that of his beloved.

(*b*) During a summer vacation a schoolteacher, a poor but excellent young man, courted the daughter of a summer resident, until the girl fell passionately in love with him, and even prevailed upon her family to countenance the matrimonial alliance in spite of the difference in position and race. One day, however, the teacher wrote his brother a letter in which he said: "Pretty, the lass is not at all, but she is very amiable, and so far so good. But whether I can make up my mind to marry a Jewess I cannot yet tell." This letter got into the hands of the fiancée, who put an end to the engagement, while at the same time his brother was wondering at the protestations of love directed to him. My informer assured me that this was really an error and not a cunning trick.

I am familiar with another case in which a woman who was dissatisfied with her old physician, and still did not openly wish to discharge him, accomplished this purpose through the interchange of letters. Here, at least, I can assert confidently that it was error and not conscious cunning that made use of this familiar comedy-motive.

(*c*) Brill[63] tells of a woman who, inquiring about a mutual friend, erroneously called her by her maiden name. Her attention having been directed to this error, she had to admit that she disliked her friend's husband and had never been satisfied with her marriage.

Maeder[64] relates a good example of how a reluctantly repressed wish can be satisfied by means of an "error." A colleague wanted to enjoy his day of leave of absence absolutely undisturbed, but he also felt that he ought to go to Lucerne to pay a call which he did not anticipate with any pleasure. After long reflection, however, he concluded to go. For pastime on the train he read the daily newspapers. He journeyed from Zurich to Arth Goldau, where he changed trains for Lucerne, all the time engrossed in reading. Presently the conductor informed him that he was in the wrong train—that is, he had got into the one which was returning from Goldau to Zurich, whereas his ticket was for Lucerne.

A very similar trick was played by me quite recently. I had promised my oldest brother to pay him a long-due visit at a sea-shore in England; as the time was short I felt obliged to travel by the shortest route and without interruption. I begged for a day's sojourn in Holland, but he thought that I could stop there on my return trip. Accordingly I journeyed from Munich through Cologne to Rotterdam—Hook of Holland—where I was to take the steamer at midnight to Harwich. In Cologne I had to change cars; I left my train to go into the Rotterdam express, but it was not to be found. I asked various railway employees, was sent from one platform to another, got into an exaggerated state of despair, and could easily reckon that during this fruitless search I had probably missed my connection.

After this was corroborated, I pondered whether or not I should spend the night in Cologne. This was favoured by a feeling of piety, for according to an old family tradition, my ancestors were once expelled from this city during a persecution of the Jews. But eventually I came to another decision; I took a later train to Rotterdam, where I arrived late at night and was thus compelled to spend a day in Holland. This brought me the fulfilment of a long-fostered wish—the sight of the beautiful Rembrandt paintings at The Hague and in the Royal Museum at Amsterdam. Not before the next forenoon, while collecting my impressions during the railway journey in England, did I definitely remember that only a few steps from the place where I got off at the railroad station in Cologne, indeed, on the same platform, I had seen a large sign, "Rotterdam—Hook of Holland." There stood the train in which I should have continued my journey.

If one does not wish to assume that, contrary to my brother's orders, I had really resolved to admire the Rembrandt pictures on my way to him, then the fact that despite clear directions I hurried away and looked for another train must be designated as an incomprehensible "blinding." Everything else—my well-acted perplexity, the emergence of the pious intention to spend the night in Cologne—was only a contrivance to hide my resolution until it had been fully accomplished.

One may possibly be disinclined to consider the class of errors which I have here explained as very numerous or particularly significant. But I leave it to your consideration whether there is no ground for extending the same points of view also to the more important errors of judgment, as evinced by people in life and science. Only for the most select and most balanced minds does it seem possible to guard the perceived picture of external reality against the distortion to which it is otherwise subjected in its transit through the psychic individuality of the one perceiving it.

***

XI

COMBINED FAULTY ACTS

Two of the last-mentioned examples, my error which transfers the Medici to Venice and that of the young man who knew how to circumvent a command against a conversation on the telephone with his lady love, have really not been fully discussed, as after careful consideration they may be shown to represent a union of forgetting with an error. I can show the same union still more clearly in certain other examples.

(*a*) A friend related to me the following experience: "Some years ago I consented to be elected to the committee of a certain literary society, as I supposed the organization might some time be of use to me in assisting me in the production of my drama. Although not much interested, I attended the meetings regularly every Friday. Some months ago I was definitely assured that one of my dramas would be presented at the theatre in F., and since that time it regularly happened that I forgot the meeting of the association. As I read their programme announcements I was ashamed of my forgetfulness. I reproached myself, feeling that it was certainly rude of me to stay away now when I no longer needed them, and determined that I would certainly not forget the next Friday. Continually I reminded myself of this resolution until the hour came and I stood before the door of the meeting-room. To my astonishment it was locked; the meeting was already over. I had mistaken my day; it was already Saturday!"

(*b*) The next example is the combination of a symptomatic action with a case of mislaying; it reached me by remote byways, but from a reliable source.

A woman travelled to Rome with her brother-in-law, a renowned artist. The visitor was highly honoured by the German residents of Rome, and among other things received a gold medal of antique origin. The woman was grieved that her brother-in-law did not sufficiently appreciate the value of this beautiful gift. After she had returned home she discovered in unpacking that—without knowing how—she had brought the medal home with her. She immediately notified her brother-in-law of this by letter, and informed him that she would send it back to Rome the next day. The next day, however, the medal was so aptly mislaid that it could not be found and could not be sent back, and then it dawned on the woman what her "absent-mindedness" signified—namely, that she wished to keep the medal herself.

(*c*) Here are some cases in which the falsified action persistently repeats itself, and at the same time also changes its mode of action:—
Due to unknown motives, Jones[65] left a letter for several days on his desk, forgetting each time to post it. He ultimately posted it, but it was returned to him from the Dead-letter Office because he forgot to address it. After addressing and posting it a second time it was again returned to him, this time without a stamp. He was then forced to recognize the unconscious opposition to the sending of the letter.

(*d*) A short account by Dr. Karl Weiss (Vienna)[66] of a case of forgetting impressively describes the futile effort to accomplish something in the face of opposition. "How persistently the unconscious activity can achieve its purpose if it has cause to prevent a resolution from being executed, and how difficult it is to guard against this tendency, will be illustrated by the following incident: An acquaintance requested me to lend him a book and bring it to him the next day. I immediately promised it, but perceived a distinct feeling of displeasure which I could not explain at the time. Later it became clear to me: this acquaintance had owed me for years a sum of money which he evidently had no intention of returning. I did not give this matter any more thought, but I recalled it the following forenoon with the same feeling of displeasure, and at once said to myself: 'Your unconscious will see to it that you forget the book, but you don't wish to appear unobliging and will therefore do everything not to forget it.' I came home, wrapped the book in paper, and put it near me on the desk while I wrote some letters.

"A little later I went away, but after a few steps I recollected that I had left on the desk the letters which I wished to post. (By the way, one of the letters was written to a person who urged me to undertake something disagreeable.) I returned, took the letters, and again left. While in the street-car it occurred to me that I had undertaken to purchase something for my wife, and I was pleased at the thought that it would be only a small package. The association, 'small package,' suddenly recalled 'book'—and only then I noticed that I did not have the book with me. Not only had I forgotten it when I left my home the first time, but I had overlooked it again when I got the letters near which it lay."

(*e*) A similar mechanism is shown in the following fully analysed observation of Otto Rank[67]:—

"A scrupulously orderly and pedantically precise man reported the following occurrence, which he considered quite remarkable: One afternoon on the street wishing to find out the time, he discovered that he had left his watch at home, an omission which to his knowledge had never occurred before. As he had an engagement elsewhere and had not enough time to return for his watch, he made use of a visit to a woman friend to borrow her watch for the evening. This was the most convenient way out of the dilemma, as he had a previous engagement to visit this lady the next day. Accordingly, he promised to return her watch at that time.

"But the following day when about to consummate this he found to his surprise that he had left the watch at home; his own watch he had with him. He then firmly resolved to return the lady's property that same afternoon, and even followed out his resolution. But on wishing to see the time on leaving her he found to his chagrin and astonishment that he had again forgotten to take his own watch.

"The repetition of this faulty action seemed so pathologic to this order-loving man that he was quite anxious to know its psychologic motivation, and when questioned whether he experienced anything disagreeable on the critical day of the first forgetting, and in what connection it had occurred, the motive was promptly found. He related that he had conversed with his mother after luncheon, shortly before leaving the house. She told him that an irresponsible relative, who had already caused him much worry and loss of money, had pawned his (the relative's) watch, and, as it was needed in the house, the relative had asked for money to redeem it. This almost "forced" loan affected our man very painfully and brought back to his memory all the disagreeable episodes perpetrated by this relative for many years.

"His symptomatic action therefore proves to be manifoldly determined. First, it gives expression to a stream of thought which runs perhaps as follows: 'I won't allow my money to be extorted this way, and if a watch is needed I will leave my own at home.' But as he needed it for the evening to keep his appointment, this intention could only be brought about on an unconscious path in the form of a symptomatic action. Second, the forgetting expresses a sentiment something like the following: 'This everlasting sacrificing of money for this good-for-nothing is bound to ruin me altogether, so that I will have to give up everything.' Although the anger, according to the report of this man, was only momentary, the repetition of the same symptomatic action conclusively shows that in the unconscious it continued to act more intensely, and may be equivalent to the conscious expression: 'I cannot get this story out of my head.[68] That the lady's watch should later meet the same fate will not surprise us after knowing this attitude of the unconscious.'

"Yet there may be still other special motives which favour the transference on the 'innocent' lady's watch. The nearest motive is probably that he would have liked to keep it as a substitute for his own sacrificed watch, and that hence he forgot to return it the next day. He also might have liked to possess this watch as a souvenir of the lady. Moreover, the forgetting of the lady's watch gave him the excuse for calling on the admired one a second time; for he was obliged to visit her in the morning in reference to another matter, and with the forgetting of the watch he seemed to indicate that this visit for which an appointment had been made so long ago was too good for him to be used simply for the return of a watch. "Twice forgetting his own watch and thus making possible the substitution of the lady's watch speaks for the fact that our man unconsciously endeavoured to avoid carrying both watches at the same time. He obviously thought of avoiding the appearance of superfluity which would have stood out in striking contrast to the want of the relative; but, on the other hand, he utilized this as a self-admonition against his apparent intention to marry this lady, reminding himself that he was tied to his family (mother) by indissoluble obligations.

"Finally, another reason for the forgetting of the lady's watch may be sought in the fact that the evening before he, a bachelor, was ashamed to be seen with a lady's watch by his friends, so that he only looked at it stealthily, and in order to evade the repetition of this painful situation he could not take the watch along. But as he was obliged to return it, there resulted here, too, an unconsciously performed symptomatic action which proved to be a compromise formation between conflicting emotional feelings and a dearly bought victory of the unconscious instance."

In the same discussion Rank has also paid attention to the very interesting relation of "faulty actions and dreams," which cannot, however, be followed here without a comprehensive analysis of the dream with which the faulty action is connected. I once dreamed at great length that I had lost my pocket-book. In the morning while dressing I actually missed it; while undressing the night before the dream I had forgotten to take it out of my trousers pocket and put it in its usual place. This forgetting was therefore not unknown to me; probably it was to give expression to an unconscious thought which was ready to appear in the dream content.

I do not mean to assert that such cases of combined faulty actions can teach anything new that we have not already seen in the individual cases. But this change in form of the faulty action, which nevertheless attains the same result, gives the plastic impression of a will working towards a definite end, and in a far more energetic way contradicts the idea that the faulty action represents something fortuitous and requires no explanation. Not less remarkable is the fact that the conscious intention thoroughly fails to check the success of the faulty action. Despite all, my friend did not pay his visit to the meeting of the literary society, and the woman found it impossible to give up the medal. That unconscious something which worked against these resolutions found another outlet after the first road was closed to it. It requires something other than the conscious counter-resolution to overcome the unknown motive; it requires a psychic work which makes the unknown known to consciousness.

***

XII

DETERMINISM—CHANCE—AND SUPERSTITIOUS BELIEFS

POINTS OF VIEW.

As the general result of the preceding separate discussions we must put down the following principle: *Certain inadequacies of our psychic capacities—whose common character will soon be more definitely determined—and certain performances which are apparently unintentional prove to be well motivated when subjected to the psychoanalytic investigation, and are determined through the consciousness of unknown motives.*

In order to belong to this class of phenomena thus explained a faulty psychic action must satisfy the following conditions:—

(*a*) It must not exceed a certain measure, which is firmly established through our estimation, and is designated by the expression "within normal limits."

(*b*) It must evince the character of the momentary and temporary disturbance. The same action must have been previously performed more correctly or we must always rely on ourselves to perform it more correctly; if we are corrected by others we must immediately recognize the truth of the correction and the incorrectness of our psychic action.

(*c*) If we at all perceive a faulty action, we must not perceive in ourselves any motivation of the same, but must attempt to explain it through "inattention" or attribute it to an "accident."

Thus there remain in this group the cases of forgetting and the errors, despite better knowledge, the lapses in speaking, reading, writing, the erroneously carried-out actions, and the so-called chance actions. The explanations of these so definite psychic processes are connected with a series of observations which may in part arouse further interest.

I. By abandoning a part of our psychic capacity as unexplainable through purposive ideas we ignore the realms of determinism in our mental life. Here, as in still other spheres, determinism reaches farther than we suppose. In the year 1900 I read an essay published in the *Zeit* written by the literary historian R. M. Meyer, in which he maintains, and illustrates by examples, that it is impossible to compose nonsense intentionally and arbitrarily. For some time I have been aware that it is impossible to think of a number, or even of a name, of one's own free will. If one investigates this seeming voluntary formation, let us say, of a number of many digits uttered in unrestrained mirth, it always proves to be so strictly determined that the determination seems impossible. I will now briefly discuss an example of an "arbitrarily chosen" first name, and then exhaustively analyse an analogous example of a "thoughtlessly uttered" number.

While preparing the history of one of my patients for publication I considered what first name I should give her in the article. There seemed to be a wide choice; of course, certain names were at once excluded by me, in the first place the real name, then the names of members of my family to which I would have objected, also some female names having an especially peculiar pronunciation. But, excluding these, there should have been no need of being puzzled about such a name. It would be thought, and I myself supposed, that a whole multitude of feminine names would be placed at my disposal. Instead of this only one sprang up, no other besides it; it was the name Dora.

I inquired as to its determination: "Who else is called Dora?" I wished to reject the next idea as incredulous; it occurred to me that the nurse of my sister's children was named Dora. But I possess so much self-control, or practice in analysis, if you like, that I held firmly to the idea and proceeded. Then a slight incident of the previous evening soon flashed through my mind which brought the looked-for determination. On my sister's dining-room table I noticed a letter bearing the address, "Miss Rosa W." Astonished, I asked whose name this was, and was informed that the right name of the supposed Dora was really Rosa, and that on accepting the position she had to lay aside her name, because Rosa would also refer to my sister. I said pityingly, "Poor people! They cannot even retain their own names!" I now recall that on hearing this I became quiet for a moment and began to think of all sorts of serious matters which merged into the obscure, but which I could now easily bring into my consciousness. Thus when I sought a name for a person *who could not retain her own name* no other except "Dora" occurred to me. The exclusiveness here is based, moreover, on firmer internal associations, for in the history of my patient it was a stranger in the house, the governess, who exerted a decisive influence on the course of the treatment.

This slight incident found its unexpected continuation many years later. While discussing in a lecture the long-since published history of the girl called Dora it occurred to me that one of my two women pupils had the very name Dora which I was obliged to utter so often in the different associations of the case. I turned to the young student, whom I knew personally, with the apology that I had really not thought that she bore the same name, and that I was ready to substitute it in my lecture by another name.

I was now confronted with the task of rapidly choosing another name, and reflected that I must not now choose the first name of the other woman student, and so set a poor example to the class, who were already quite conversant with psychoanalysis. I was therefore well pleased when the name "Erna" occurred to me as the substitute for Dora, and Erna I used in the discourse. After the lecture I asked myself whence the name "Erna" could possibly have originated, and had to laugh as I observed that the feared possibility in the choice of the substitutive name had come to pass, in part at least. The other lady's family name was Lucerna, of which Erna was a part.

In a letter to a friend I informed him that I had finished reading the proof-sheets of *The Interpretation of Dreams*, and that I did not intend to make any further changes in it, "even if it contained *2,467* mistakes." I immediately attempted to explain to myself the number, and added this little analysis as a postscript to the letter. It will be best to quote it now as I wrote it when I caught myself in this transaction:—

"I will add hastily another contribution to the Psychopathology of Everyday Life. You will find in the letter the number 2,467 as a jocose and arbitrary estimation of the number of errors that may be found in the dream-book. I meant to write: no matter how large the number might be, and this one presented itself. But there is nothing arbitrary or undetermined in the psychic life. You will therefore rightly suppose that the unconscious hastened to determine the number which was liberated by consciousness. Just previous to this I had read in the paper that General E. M. had been retired as Inspector-General of Ordnance. You must know that I am interested in this man. While I was serving as military medical student he, then a colonel, once came into the hospital and said to the physician: 'You must make me well in eight days, as I have some work to do for which the Emperor is waiting.'

"At that time I decided to follow this man's career, and just think, to-day (1899) he is at the end of it—Inspector-General of Ordnance and already retired. I wished to figure out in what time he had covered this road, and assumed that I had seen him in the hospital in 1882. That would make 17 years. I related this to my wife, and she remarked, 'Then you, too, should be retired.' And I protested, 'The Lord forbid!' After this conversation I seated myself at the table to write to you. The previous train of thought continued, and for good reason. The figuring was incorrect; I had a definite recollection of the circumstances in my mind. I had celebrated my coming of age, my *24th* birthday, in the military prison (for being absent without permission). Therefore I must have seen him in 1880, which makes it 19 years ago. You then have the number 24 in 2,467! Now take the number that represents my age, 43, and add 24 years to it and you get *67*! That is, to the question whether I wished to retire I had expressed the wish to work 24 years more. Obviously I am annoyed that in the interval during which I followed Colonel M. I have not accomplished much myself, and still there is a sort of triumph in the fact that he is already finished, while I still have all before me. Thus we may justly say that not even the unintentionally thrown-out number 2,467 lacks its determination from the unconscious."

Since this first example of the interpretation of an apparently arbitrary choice of a number I have repeated a similar test with the same result; but most cases are of such intimate content that they do not lend themselves to report.

It is for this reason that I shall not hesitate to add here a very interesting analysis of a "chance number" which Dr. Alfred Adler (Vienna) received from a "perfectly healthy" man.[69] A. wrote to me: "Last night I devoted myself to the *Psychopathology of Everyday* Life, and I would have read it all through had I not been hindered by a remarkable coincidence. When I read that every number that we apparently conjure up quite arbitrarily in our consciousness has a definite meaning, I decided to test it. The number 1,734 occurred to my mind. The following associations then came up: 1,734 ÷ 17 = 102; 102 ÷ 17 = 6. I then separated the number into 17 and 34. I am 34 years old. I believe that I once told you that I consider 34 the last year of youth, and for this reason I felt miserable on my last birthday. The end of my 17th year was the beginning of a very nice and interesting period of my development. I divide my life into periods of 17 years. What do the divisions signify? The number 102 recalls the fact that volume 102 of the Reclam Universal Library is Kotzebue's play *Menschenhass und Reue* (*Human Hatred and Repentance*).

"My present psychic state is 'human hatred and repentance.' No. 6 of the U. L. (I know a great many numbers by heart) is Mullner's 'Schuld' (Fault). I am constantly annoyed at the thought that it is through my own fault that I have not become what I could have been with my abilities.

"I then asked myself, 'What is No. 17 of the U. L.?' But I could not recall it. But as I positively knew it before, I assumed that I wished to forget this number. All reflection was in vain. I wished to continue with my reading, but I read only mechanically without understanding a word, for I was annoyed by the number 17. I extinguished the light and continued my search. It finally came to me that number 17 must be a play by Shakespeare. But which one? I thought of Hero and Leander. Apparently a stupid attempt of my will to distract me. I finally arose and consulted the catalogue of the U. L. Number 17 was *Macbeth*! To my surprise I had to discover that I knew nothing of the play, despite the fact that it did not interest me any less than any other Shakespearean drama. I only thought of: murder, Lady Macbeth, witches, 'nice is ugly,' and that I found Schiller's version of *Macbeth* very nice. Undoubtedly I also wished to forget the play. Then it occurred to me that 17 and 34 may be divided by 17 and result in 1 and 2. Numbers 1 and 2 of the U. L. is Goethe's *Faust*. Formerly I found much of Faust in me."

We must regret that the discretion of the physician did not allow us to see the significance of ideas. Adler remarked that the man did not succeed in the synthesis of his analysis. His association would hardly be worth reporting unless their continuation would bring out something that would give us the key to the understanding of the number 1,734 and the whole series of ideas.

To quote further: "To be sure this morning I had an experience which speaks much for the correctness of the Freudian conception. My wife, whom I awakened through my getting up at night, asked me what I wanted with the catalogue of the U. L. I told her the story. She found it all pettifogging but—very interesting. *Macbeth*, which caused me so much trouble, she simply passed over. She said that nothing came to her mind when she thought of a number. I answered, 'Let us try it.' She named the number 117. To this I immediately replied: '17 refers to what I just told you; furthermore, I told you yesterday that if a wife is in the 82nd year and the husband is in the 35th year it must be a gross misunderstanding.' For the last few days I have been teasing my wife by maintaining that she was a little old mother of 82 years. 82 + 35 = 117."

The man who did not know how to determine his own number at once found the solution when his wife named a number which was apparently arbitrarily chosen. As a matter of fact, the woman understood very well from which complex the number of her husband originated, and chose her own number from the same complex, which was surely common to both, as it dealt in his case with their relative ages. Now, we find it easy to interpret the number that occurred to the man. As Dr. Adler indicates, it expressed a repressed wish of the husband which, fully developed, would read: "For a man of 34 years as I am, only a woman of 17 would be suitable."

Lest one should think too lightly of such "playing," I will add that I was recently informed by Dr. Adler that a year after the publication of this analysis the man was divorced from his wife.[70]

Adler gives a similar explanation for the origin of obsessive numbers. Also the choice of so-called "favourite numbers" is not without relation to the life of the person concerned, and does not lack a certain psychologic interest. A gentleman who evinced a particular partiality for the numbers 17 and 19 could specify, after brief reflection, that at the age of 17 he attained the greatly longed-for academic freedom by having been admitted to the university, that at 19 he made his first long journey, and shortly thereafter made his first scientific discovery. But the fixation of this preference followed later, after two questionable affairs, when the same numbers were invested with importance in his "love-life."

Indeed, even those numbers which we use in a particular connection extremely often and with apparent arbitrariness can be traced by analysis to an unexpected meaning. Thus, one day it struck one of my patients that he was particularly fond of saying, "I have already told you this from 17 to 36 times." And he asked himself whether there was any motive for it. It soon occurred to him that he was born on the 27th day of the month, and that his younger brother was born on the 26th day of another month, and he had grounds for complaint that Fate had robbed him of so many of the benefits of life only to bestow them on his younger brother. Thus he represented this partiality of Fate by deducting 10 from the date of his birth and adding it to the date of his brother's birthday. I am the elder and yet am so "cut short."

I shall tarry a little longer at the analysis of chance numbers, for I know of no other individual observation which would so readily demonstrate the existence of highly organized thinking processes of which consciousness has no knowledge. Moreover, there is no better example of analysis in which the suggestion of the position, a frequent accusation, is so distinctly out of consideration. I shall therefore report the analysis of a chance number of one of my patients (with his consent), to which I will only add that he is the youngest of many children and that he lost his beloved father in his young years.

While in a particularly happy mood he let the number *426,718* come to his mind, and put to himself the question, "Well, what does it bring to your mind?" First came a joke he had heard: "If your catarrh of the nose is treated by a doctor it lasts 42 days, if it is not treated it lasts—6 weeks." This corresponds to the first digit of the number (42 = 6 × 7). During the obstruction that followed this first solution I called his attention to the fact that the number of six digits selected by him contains all the first numbers except 3 and 5. He at once found the continuation of this solution:—

"We were altogether 7 children, I was the youngest. Number 3 in the order of the children corresponds to my sister A., and 5 to my brother L.; both of them were my enemies. As a child I used to pray to the Lord every night that He should take out of my life these two tormenting spirits. It seems to me that I have fulfilled for myself this wish: '3' and '5,' the *evil* brother and the hated sister, are omitted."

"If the number stands for your sisters and brothers, what significance is there to 18 at the end? You were altogether only 7."

"I often thought if my father had lived longer I should not have been the youngest child. If one more would have come, we should have been 8, and there would have been a younger child, toward whom I could have played the rôle of the older one."

With this the number was explained, but we still wished to find the connection between the first part of the interpretation and the part following it. This came very readily from the condition required for the last digits—if the father had lived longer. 42 = 6 × 7 signifies the ridicule directed against the doctors who could not help the father, and in this way expresses the wish for the continued existence of the father. The whole number really corresponds to the fulfilment of his two wishes in reference to his family circle—namely, that both the evil brother and sister should die and that another little child should follow him. Or, briefly expressed: *If only these two had died in place of my father!*[71]

Another analysis of numbers I take from Jones.[72] A gentleman of his acquaintance let the number 986 come to his mind, and defied him to connect it to anything of special interest in his mind. "Six years ago, on the hottest day he could remember, he had seen a joke in an evening newspaper, which stated that the thermometer had stood at 98.6° F., evidently an exaggeration of 98.6° F. We were at the time seated in front of a very hot fire, from which he had just drawn back, and he remarked, probably quite correctly, that the heat had aroused his dormant memory. However, I was curious to know why this memory had persisted with such vividness as to be so readily brought out, for with most people it surely would have been forgotten beyond recall, unless it had become associated with some other mental experience of more significance.

"He told me that on reading the joke he had laughed uproariously, and that on many subsequent occasions he had recalled it with great relish. As the joke was obviously of an exceedingly tenuous nature, this strengthened my expectation that more lay behind. His next thought was the general reflection that the conception of heat had always greatly impressed him, that heat was the most important thing in the universe, the source of all life, and so on. This remarkable attitude of a quite prosaic young man certainly needed some explanation, so I asked him to continue his free associations. The next thought was of a factory stack which he could see from his bedroom window. He often stood of an evening watching the flame and smoke issuing out of it, and reflecting on this deplorable waste of energy. Heat, flame, the source of life, the waste of vital energy issuing from an upright, hollow tube—it was not hard to divine from such associations that the ideas of heat and fire were unconsciously linked in his mind with the idea of love, as is so frequent in symbolic thinking, and that there was a strong masturbation complex present, a conclusion that he presently confirmed."

Those who wish to get a good impression of the way the material of numbers becomes elaborated in the unconscious thinking, I refer to two papers by Jung[73] and Jones.[74]

In personal analysis of this kind two things were especially striking. First, the absolute somnambulistic certainty with which I attacked the unknown objective point, merging into a mathematical train of thought, which later suddenly extended to the looked-for number, and the rapidity with which the entire subsequent work was performed. Secondly, the fact that the numbers were always at the disposal of my unconscious mind, when as a matter of fact I am a poor mathematician and find it very difficult to consciously recall years, house numbers, and the like. Moreover, in these unconscious mental operations with figures I found a tendency to superstition, the origin of which had long remained unknown to me.

It will not surprise us to find that not only numbers but also mental occurrences of different kinds of words regularly prove on analytic investigation to be well determined.

Brill relates: "While working on the English edition of this book I was obsessed one morning with the strange word 'Cardillac.' Busily intent on my work, I refused at first to pay attention to it, but, as is usually the case, I simply could not do anything else. 'Cardillac' was constantly in my mind. Realizing that my refusal to recognize it was only a resistance, I decided to analyse it. The following associations occurred to me: *Cardillac*, *cardiac*, *carrefour*, *Cadillac.*

"*Cardiac* recalled cardalgia—heartache—a medical friend who had recently told me confidentially that he feared that he had some cardiac affection because he had suffered some attacks of pain in the region of his heart. Knowing him so well, I at once rejected his theory, and told him that his attacks were of a neurotic character, and that his other apparent physical ailments were also only the expression of his neurosis.

"I might add that just before telling me of his heart trouble he spoke of a business matter of vital interest to him which had suddenly come to naught. Being a man of unbounded ambitions, he was very depressed because of late he had suffered many similar reverses. His neurotic conflicts, however, had become manifest a few months before this misfortune. Soon after his father's death had left a big business on his hands. As the business could be continued only under my friend's management, he was unable to decide whether to enter into commercial life or continue his chosen career. His great ambition was to become a successful medical practitioner, and although he had practised medicine successfully for many years, he was not altogether satisfied with the financial fluctuations of his professional income. On the other hand, his father's business promised him an assured, though limited, return. In brief, he was 'at a crossing and did not know which way to turn.'

"I then recalled the word *carrefour*, which is the French for 'crossing,' and it occurred to me that while working in a hospital in Paris I lived near the 'Carrefour St. Lazarre.' And now I could understand what relation all these associations had for me.

"When I resolved to leave the State Hospital I made the decision, first, because I desired to get married, and, secondly, because I wished to enter private practice. This brought up a new problem. Although my State hospital service was an absolute success, judging by promotions and so on, I felt like a great many others in the same situation, namely, that my training was ill suited for private practice. To specialize in mental work was a daring undertaking for one without money and social connections. I also felt that the best I could do for patients should they ever come my way would be to commit them to one of the hospitals, as I had little confidence in the home treatment in vogue. In spite of the enormous advances made in recent years in mental work, the specialist is almost helpless when he is confronted with the average case of insanity. This may be partially attributed to the fact that such cases are brought to him after they have fully developed the psychosis when hospital treatment is imperative. Of the great army of milder mental disturbances, the so-called border-line cases, which make up the bulk of clinic and private work and which rightfully belong to the mental specialist, I knew very little, as those patients rarely, or never, came to the State hospital, and what I did know concerning the treatment of neurasthenia and psychasthenia was not conducive to make me more hopeful of success in private practice.

"It was in this state of mind that I came to Paris, where I hoped to learn enough about the psychoneuroses to enable me to continue my specialty in private practice, and yet feel that I could do something for my patients. What I saw in Paris did not, however, help to change my state of mind. There, too, most of the work was directed to dead tissues. The mental aspects, as such, received but scant attention. I was, therefore, seriously thinking of giving up my mental work for some other specialty. As can be seen, I was confronted with a situation similar to the one of my medical friend. I, too, was at a crossing and did not know which way to turn. My suspense was soon ended. One day I received a letter from my friend Professor Peterson, who, by the way, was responsible for my entering the State hospital service. In this letter he advised me not to give up my work, and suggested the psychiatric clinic of Zurich, where he thought I could find what I desired.

"But what does *Cadillac* mean? Cadillac is the name of a hotel and of an automobile. A few days before in a country place my medical friend and I had been trying to hire an automobile, but there was none to be had. We both expressed the wish to own an automobile—again an unrealized ambition. I also recalled that the 'Carrefour St. Lazarre' always impressed me as being one of the busiest thoroughfares in Paris. It was always congested with automobiles. Cadillac also recalled that only a few days ago on the way to my clinic I noticed a large sign over a building which announced that on a certain day 'this building was to be occupied by the Cadillac,' etc. This at first made me think of the Cadillac Hotel, but on second sight I noticed that it referred to the Cadillac motor-car. There was a sudden obstruction here for a few moments. The word Cadillac reappeared and by sound association the word *catalogue* occurred to me. This word brought back a very mortifying occurrence of recent origin, the motive of which is again blighted ambition.

"When one wishes to report any auto-analysis he must be prepared to lay bare many intimate affairs of his own life. Any one reading carefully Professor Freud's works cannot fail to become intimately acquainted with him and his family. I have often been asked by persons who claim to have read and studied Freud's works such questions as: 'How old is Freud?' 'Is Freud married?' 'How many children has he?' etc. Whenever I hear these or similar questions I know that the questioner has either lied when he made these assertions, or, to be more charitable, that he is a very careless and superficial reader. All these questions and many more are answered in Freud's works. Auto-analyses are autobiographies *par excellence*; but whereas the autobiographer may for definite reasons consciously and unconsciously hide many facts of his life, the auto-analyst not only tells the truth consciously, but perforce brings to light his whole intimate personality. It is for these reasons that one finds it very unpleasant to report his own auto-analyses. However, as we often report our patients' unconscious productions, it is but fair that we should sacrifice ourselves on the altar of publicity when occasion demands. This is my apology for having thrust some of my personal affairs on the reader, and for being obliged to continue a little longer in the same strain.

"Before digressing with the last remarks I mentioned that the word *Cadillac* brought the sound association *catalogue*. This association brought back another important epoch in my life with which Professor Peterson is connected. Last May I was informed by the secretary of the faculty that I was appointed chief of clinic of the department of psychiatry. I need hardly say that I was exceedingly pleased to be so honoured—in the first place because it was the realization of an ambition which I dared entertain only under special euphoric states; and, secondly, it was a compensation for the many unmerited criticisms from those who are blindly and unreasonably opposing some of my work. Soon thereafter I called on the stenographer of the faculty and spoke to her about a correction to be made in my name as it was printed in the catalogue. For some unknown reason (perhaps racial prejudice) this stenographer, a maiden lady, must have taken a dislike to me. For about three years I repeatedly requested her to have this correction made, but she had paid no attention to me. To be sure she always promised to attend to it, but the mistake remained uncorrected.

"When I saw her last May I again reminded her of this correction, and also called her attention to the fact that as I had been appointed chief of clinic I was especially anxious to have my name correctly printed in the catalogue. She apologized for her remissness and assured me that everything should be as I requested. Imagine my surprise and chagrin when on receiving the new catalogue I found that while the correction had been made in my name I was not listed as chief of clinic. When I asked her about this she was quite puzzled; she said she had no idea that I had been appointed chief of clinic. She had to consult the minutes of the faculty, written by herself, before she was convinced of it. It should be noted that as recorder to the faculty it was her duty to know all these things as soon as they transpired.[75] When she finally ascertained that I was right she was very apologetic and informed me that she would at once write to the superintendent of the clinic to inform him of my appointment, something which she should have done months before. Of course I gained nothing by her regrets and apologies. The catalogue was published and those who read it did not find my name in the desired place. I am chief of clinic in fact but not in name. Moreover, as the appointments are made only for one year, it is quite likely that my great ambition will never be actually realized.

"Thus the obsessive neologism *cardillac*, which is a condensation of *cardiac*, *Cadillac*, and *catalogue*, contains some of the most important efforts of my medical experience. When I was almost at the end of this analysis I suddenly recalled a dream containing this neologism cardillac in which my wish was realized. My name appeared in its rightful place in the catalogue. The person who showed it to me in the dream was

Professor Peterson. It was when I was at the first 'crossing' after I had graduated from the medical college that Professor Peterson urged me to enter the hospital service. About five years later while I was in the state of indecision which I have described, it was Professor Peterson who advised me to go to the clinic of psychiatry at Zurich where through Bleuler and Jung I first became acquainted with Professor Freud and his works, and it was also through the kind recommendation of Dr. Peterson that I was elevated to my present position."

I am indebted to Dr. Hitschman for the solution of another case in which a line of poetry repeatedly obtruded itself on the mind in a certain place without showing any trace of its origin and relation.

Related by Dr. E.: "Six years ago I travelled from Biarritz to San Sebastian. The railroad crosses over the Bidassao—a river which here forms the boundary between France and Spain. On the bridge one has a splendid view, on the one side of the broad valley and the Pyrenees and on the other of the sea. It was a beautiful, bright summer day; everything was filled with sun and light. I was on a vacation and pleased with my trip to Spain. Suddenly the following words came to me: '*But the soul is already free, floating on a sea of light.*'

"At that time I was trying to remember where these lines came from, but I could not remember; judging by the rhythm, the words must be a part of some poem, which, however, entirely escaped my memory. Later when the verse repeatedly came to my mind, I asked many people about it without receiving any information.

"Last year I crossed the same bridge on my return journey from Spain. It was a very dark night and it rained. I looked through the window to ascertain whether we had already reached the frontier station and noticed that we were on the Bidassao bridge. Immediately the above-cited verse returned to my memory and again I could not recall its origin.

"At home many months later I found Uhland's poems. I opened the volume and my glance fell upon the verse: '*But the soul is already free, floating on a sea of light,*' which were the concluding lines of the poem entitled 'The Pilgrim.' I read the poem and dimly recalled that I had known it many years ago. The scene of action is in Spain, and this seemed to me to be the only relation between the quoted verse and the place on the railroad journey described by me. I was only half satisfied with my discovery and mechanically continued to turn the pages of the book. On turning the next page I found a poem the title of which was '*Bidassao Bridge*.'

"I may add that the contents of this poem seemed even stranger to me than that of the first, and that its first verse read:

"'On the Bidassao bridge stands a saint grey with age, he blesses to the right the Spanish mountain, to the left he blesses the French land.'"

II. This understanding of the determination of apparently arbitrarily selected names, numbers, and words may perhaps contribute to the solution of another problem. As is known, many persons argue against the assumption of an absolute psychic determinism by referring to an intense feeling of conviction that there is a free will. This feeling of conviction exists, but is not incompatible with the belief in determinism. Like all normal feelings, it must be justified by something. But, so far as I can observe, it does not manifest itself in weighty and important decisions; on these occasions one has much more the feeling of a psychic compulsion and gladly falls back upon it. (Compare Luther's "Here I stand, I cannot do anything else.")

On the other hand, it is in trivial and indifferent decisions that one feels sure that he could just as easily have acted differently, that he acted of his own free will, and without any motives. From our analyses we therefore need not contest the right of the feeling of conviction that there is a free will. If we distinguish conscious from unconscious motivation, we are then informed by the feeling of conviction that the conscious motivation does not extend over all our motor resolutions. *Minima non curat prætor.* What is thus left free from the one side receives its motive from the other side, from the unconscious, and the determinism in the psychic realm is thus carried out uninterruptedly.[76]

III. Although conscious thought must be altogether ignorant of the motivation of the faulty actions described above, yet it would be desirable to discover a psychologic proof of its existence; indeed, reasons obtained through a deeper knowledge of the unconscious make it probable that such proofs are to be discovered somewhere. As a matter of fact phenomena can be demonstrated in two spheres which seem to correspond to an unconscious and hence to a displaced knowledge of these motives.

(*a*)It is a striking and generally to be recognized feature in the behaviour of paranoiacs, that they attach the greatest significance to the trivial details in the behaviour of others. Details which are usually overlooked by others they interpret and utilize as the basis of far-reaching conclusions. For example, the last paranoiac seen by me concluded that there was a general understanding among people of his environment, because at his departure from the railway-station they made a certain motion with one hand. Another noticed how people walked on the street, how they brandished their walking-sticks, and the like.[77]

The category of the accidental, requiring no motivation, which the normal person lets pass as a part of his own psychic activities and faulty actions, is thus rejected by the paranoiac in the application to the psychic manifestations to others. All that he observes in others is full of meaning, all is explainable. But how does he come to look at it in this manner? Probably here as in so many other cases, he projects into the mental life of others what exists in his own unconscious activity. Many things obtrude themselves on consciousness in paranoia which in normal and neurotic persons can only be demonstrated through psychoanalysis as existing in their unconscious.[78] In a certain sense the paranoiac is here justified, he perceives something that escapes the normal person, he sees clearer than one of normal intellectual capacity, but his knowledge becomes worthless when he imputes to others the state of affairs he thus recognizes. I hope that I shall not be expected to justify every paranoic interpretation. But the point which we grant to paranoia in this conception of chance actions will facilitate for us the psychologic understanding of the conviction which the paranoiac attaches to all these interpretations. *There is certainly some truth to it*; even our errors of judgment, which are not designated as morbid, acquire their feeling of conviction in the same way. This feeling is justified for a certain part of the erroneous train of thought or for the source of its origin, and we shall later extend to it the remaining relationships.

(*b*) The phenomena of superstition furnish another indication of the unconscious motivation in chance and faulty actions. I will make myself clear through the discussion of a simple experience which gave me the starting-point to these reflections.

Having returned from vacation, my thoughts immediately turned to the patients with whom I was to occupy myself in the beginning of my year's work. My first visit was to a very old woman (see above) for whom I had twice daily performed the same professional services for many years. Owing to this monotony unconscious thoughts have often found expression on the way to the patient and during my occupation with her. She was over ninety years old; it was therefore pertinent to ask oneself at the beginning of each year how much longer she was likely to live.

On the day of which I speak I was in a hurry and took a carriage to her house. Every coachman at the cabstand near my house knew the old woman's address, as each of them had often driven me there. This day it happened that the driver did not stop in front of her house, but before one of the same number in a near-by and really similar-looking parallel street. I noticed the mistake and reproached the coachman, who apologized for it.

Is it of any significance when I am taken to a house where the old woman is not to be found? Certainly not to me; but were I *superstitious*, I should see an omen in this incident, a hint of fate that this would be the last year for the old woman. A great many omens which have been preserved by history have been founded on no better symbolism. Of course, I explain the incident as an accident without further meaning.

The case would have been entirely different had I come on foot and, "absorbed in thought" or "through distraction," I had gone to the house in the parallel street instead of the correct one. I would not explain that as an accident, but as an action with unconscious intent requiring interpretation. My explanation of this "lapse in walking" would probably be that I expected that the time would soon come when I should not meet the old woman any longer.

I therefore differ from a superstitious person in the following manner:—

I do not believe that an occurrence in which my mental life takes no part can teach me anything hidden concerning the future shaping of reality; but I do believe that an unintentional manifestation of my own mental activity surely contains something concealed which belongs only to my mental life—that is, I believe in outer (real) chance, but not in inner (psychic) accidents. With the superstitious person the case is reversed: he knows nothing of the motive of his chance and faulty actions, he believes in the existence of psychic contingencies; he is therefore inclined to attribute meaning to external chance, which manifests itself in actual occurrence, and to see in the accident a means of expression for something hidden outside of him. There are two differences between me and the superstitious person: first, he projects the motive to the outside, while I look for it in myself; second, he explains the accident by an event which I trace to a thought. What he considers hidden corresponds to the unconscious with me, and the compulsion not to let chance pass as chance, but to explain it as common to both of us.

Thus I admit that this conscious ignorance and unconscious knowledge of the motivation of psychic accidentalness is one of the psychic roots of superstition. *Because* the superstitious person knows nothing of the motivation of his own accidental actions, and because the fact of this motivation strives for a place in his recognition, he is compelled to dispose of them by displacing them into the outer world. If such a connection exists it can hardly be limited to this single case. As a matter of fact, I believe that a large portion of the mythological conception of the world which reaches far into the most modern religions *is nothing but psychology projected into the outer world.* The dim perception (the endo-psychic perception, as it were) of psychic factors and relations[79] of the unconscious was taken as a model in the construction of a *transcendental reality*, which is destined to be changed again by science into *psychology of the unconscious.*

It is difficult to express it in other terms; the analogy to paranoia must here come to our aid. We venture to explain in this way the myths of paradise and the fall of man, of God, of good and evil, of immortality, and the like—that is, to transform *metaphysics* into *metapsychology.* The gap between the paranoiac's displacement and that of superstition is narrower than appears at first sight. When human beings began to think, they were obviously compelled to explain the outer world in an anthropomorphic sense by a multitude of personalities in their own image; the accidents which they explained superstitiously were thus actions and expressions of persons. In that regard they behaved just like paranoiacs, who draw conclusions from insignificant signs which others give them, and like all normal persons who justly take the unintentional actions of their fellow-beings as a basis for the estimation of their characters. Only in our modern philosophical, but by no means finished, views of life does superstition seem so much out of place: in the view of life of pre-scientific times and nations it was justified and consistent.

The Roman who gave up an important undertaking because he sighted an ill-omened flock of birds was relatively right; his action was consistent with his principles. But if he withdrew from an undertaking because he had stumbled on his threshold (*un Romain retournerait*), he was absolutely superior even to us unbelievers. He was a better psychologist than we are striving to become. For his stumbling could demonstrate to him the existence of a doubt, an internal counter-current the force of which could weaken the power of his intention at the moment of its execution. For only by concentrating all psychic forces on the desired aim can one be assured of perfect success. How does Schiller's Tell, who hesitated so long to shoot the apple from his son's head, answer the bailiff's question why he had provided himself with a second arrow?

"With the second arrow I would have pierced you had I struck my dear child—and truly, I should not have failed to reach you."

IV. Whoever has had the opportunity of studying the concealed psychic feelings of persons by means of psychoanalysis can also tell something new concerning the quality of unconscious motives, which express themselves in superstition. Nervous persons afflicted with compulsive thinking and compulsive states, who are often very intelligent, show very plainly that superstition originates from repressed hostile and cruel impulses. The greater part of superstition signifies fear of impending evil, and he who has frequently wished evil to others, but because of a good bringing-up has repressed the same into the unconscious, will be particularly apt to expect punishment for such unconscious evil in the form of a misfortune threatening him from without.

If we concede that we have by no means exhausted the psychology of superstition in these remarks, we must, on the other hand, at least touch upon the question whether real roots of superstition should be altogether denied, whether there are really no omens, prophetic dreams, telepathic experiences, manifestations of supernatural forces, and the like. I am now far from willing to repudiate without anything further all these phenomena, concerning which we possess so many minute observations even from men of intellectual prominence, and which should certainly form a basis for further investigation. We may even hope that some of these observations will be explained by our present knowledge of the unconscious psychic processes without necessitating radical changes in our present aspect. If still other phenomena, as, for example, those maintained by the spiritualists, should be proven, we should then consider the modification of our "laws" as demanded by the new experience, without becoming confused in regard to the relation of things of this world.

In the sphere of these analyses I can only answer the questions here proposed subjectively—that is, in accordance with my personal experience. I am sorry to confess that I belong to that class of unworthy individuals before whom the spirits cease their activities and the supernatural disappears, so that I have never been in position to experience anything personally that would stimulate belief in the miraculous. Like everybody else, I have had forebodings and experienced misfortunes; but the two evaded each other, so that nothing followed the foreboding, and the misfortune struck me unannounced. When as a young man I lived alone in a strange city I frequently heard my name suddenly pronounced by an unmistakable, dear voice, and I then made a note of the exact moment of the hallucination in order to inquire carefully of those at home what had occurred at that time. There was nothing to it. On the other hand, I later worked among my patients calmly and without foreboding while my child almost bled to death. Nor have I ever been able to recognize as unreal phenomena any of the forebodings reported to me by my patients.

The belief in prophetic dreams numbers many adherents, because it can be supported by the fact that some things really so happen in the future as they were previously foretold by the wish of the dream. But in this there is little to be wondered at, as many far-reaching deviations may be regularly demonstrated between a dream and the fulfilment which the credulity of the dreamer prefers to neglect.

A nice example, one which may be justly called prophetic, was once brought to me for exhaustive analysis by an intelligent and truth-loving patient. She related that she once dreamed that she had met a former friend and family physician in front of a certain store in a certain street, and next morning when she went down town she actually met him at the place named in the dream. I may observe that the significance of this wonderful coincidence was not proven to be due to any subsequent event—that is, it could not be justified through future occurrences.

Careful examination definitely established the fact that there was no proof that the woman recalled the dream in the morning following the night of the dream—that is, before the walk and before the meeting. She could offer no objection when this state of affairs was presented in a manner that robbed this episode of everything miraculous, leaving only an interesting psychologic problem. One morning she had walked through this very street, had met her old family physician before that certain store, and on seeing him received the conviction that during the preceding night she had dreamed of this meeting at this place.

The analysis then showed with great probability how she came to this conviction, to which, in accordance with the general rule, we cannot deny a certain right to credence. A meeting at a definite place following a previous expectation really describes the fact of a rendezvous. The old family physician awakened her memory of old times, when meetings with a third person, also a friend of the physician, were of marked significance to her. Since that time she had continued her relations with this gentleman, and the day before the mentioned dream she had waited for him in vain. If I could report in greater detail the circumstances here before us, I could easily show that the illusion of the prophetic dream at the sight of the friend of former times is perchance equivalent to the following speech: "Ah, doctor, you now remind me of bygone times, when I never had to wait in vain for N. when we had arranged a meeting."

I have observed in myself a simple and easily explained example, which is probably a good model for similar occurrences of those familiar "remarkable coincidences" wherein we meet a person of whom we were just thinking. During a walk through the inner city a few days after the title of "Professor" was bestowed on me, which carries with it a great deal of prestige even in monarchical cities, my thoughts suddenly merged into a childish revenge-fantasy against a certain married couple. Some months previous they had called me to see their little daughter who suffered from an interesting compulsive manifestation following the appearance of a dream. I took a great interest in the case, the genesis of which I believed I could surmise, but the parents were unfavourable to my treatment, and gave me to understand that they thought of applying to a foreign authority who cured by means of hypnotism. I now fancied that after the failure of this attempt, the parents begged me to resume my treatment, that they now had full confidence in me, etc. But I answered: "Now that I have become a professor, you have confidence in me. The title has made no change in my ability; if you could not use me when I was instructor you can get along without me now that I am a professor." At this point my fantasy was interrupted by a loud "Good evening, Professor!" and as I looked up there passed me the same couple on whom I had just taken this imaginary vengeance.

The next reflection destroyed the semblance of the miraculous. I was walking towards this couple on a straight, almost deserted street; glancing up hastily at a distance of perhaps twenty steps from me, I had spied and realized their stately personalities; but this perception, following the model of a negative hallucination, was set aside by certain emotionally accentuated motives and then asserted itself in the apparently spontaneous emerging fantasy.

A similar experience is related by Brill, which also throws some light on the nature of telepathy.

"While engrossed in conversation during our customary Sunday evening dinner at one of the large New York restaurants, I suddenly stopped and irrelevantly remarked to my wife, 'I wonder how Dr. R. is doing in Pittsburg.' She looked at me much astonished and said: 'Why, that is exactly what I have been thinking for the last few seconds! Either you have transferred this thought to me or I have transferred it to you. How can you otherwise explain this strange phenomenon?' I had to admit that I could offer no solution. Our conversation throughout the dinner showed not the remotest association to Dr. R., nor, so far as our memories went, had we heard or spoken of him for some time. Being a sceptic, I refused to admit that there was anything mysterious about it, although inwardly I felt quite uncertain. To be frank, I was somewhat mystified.

"But we did not remain very long in this state of mind, for on looking toward the cloak-room we were surprised to see Dr. R. Though closer inspection showed our mistake, we were both struck by the remarkable resemblance of this stranger to Dr. R. From the position of the cloak-room we were forced to conclude that this stranger had passed our table. Absorbed in our conversation, we had not noticed him consciously, but the visual image had stirred up the association of his double, Dr. R. That we should both have experienced the same thought is also quite natural. The last word from our friend was to the effect that he had taken up private practice in Pittsburg, and, being aware of the vicissitudes that beset the beginner, it was quite natural to wonder how fortune smiled upon him.

"What promised to be a supernatural manifestation was thus easily explained on a normal basis; but had we not noticed the stranger before he left the restaurant, it would have been impossible to exclude the mysterious. I venture to say that such simple mechanisms are at the bottom of the most complicated telepathic manifestations; at least, such has been my experience in all cases accessible to investigation."

Another "solution of an apparent foreboding" was reported by Otto Rank[80]:—

"Some time ago I had experienced a remarkable variation of that 'peculiar coincidence' wherein one meets a person who has just been occupying one's thoughts. Shortly before Christmas I went to the Austro-Hungarian Bank in order to obtain ten new silver crown-pieces destined for Christmas gifts. Absorbed in ambitious fantasies which dealt with the contrast of my meagre means to the enormous sums in the banking-house, I turned into the narrow street to the bank. In front of the door I saw an automobile and many people going in and out. I thought to myself: 'The officials will have plenty of time for my new crowns; naturally I shall be quick about it; I shall put down the paper notes to be exchanged, and say, "Please give me gold."' I realized my mistake at once—I was to have asked for *silver*—and awoke from my fantasies.

"I was now only a few steps from the entrance, and noticed a young man coming toward me who looked familiar, but whom

I could not definitely identify on account of my short-sightedness. As he came nearer I recognized him as a classmate of my brother whose name was *Gold* and from whose brother, a well-known journalist, I had great expectations in the beginning of my literary career. But these expectations had not materialized, and with them had vanished the hoped-for material success with which my fantasies were occupying themselves on my way to the bank. Thus engrossed I must have unconsciously perceived the approach of Mr. Gold, who impressed himself on my conscience while I was dreaming of material success, and thereby caused me to ask the cashier for gold instead of the inferior silver. But, on the other hand, the paradoxical fact that my unconscious was able to perceive an object long before it was recognized by the eye might in part be explained by the complex readiness (*Komplexbereitschaft*) of Bleuler. For my mind was attuned to the material, and, contrary to my better knowledge, it guided my steps from the very beginning to buildings where gold and paper money were exchanged."

To the category of the wonderful and uncanny we may also add that strange feeling we perceive in certain moments and situations when it seems as if we had already had exactly the same experience, or had previously found ourselves in the same situation. Yet we are never successful in our efforts to recall clearly those former experiences and situations. I know that I follow only the loose colloquial expression when I designate that which stimulates us in such moments as a "feeling." We undoubtedly deal with a judgment, and, indeed, with a judgment of cognition; but these cases, nevertheless, have a character peculiar to themselves, and besides, we must not ignore the fact that we never recall what we are seeking.

I do not know whether this phenomenon of *Déjà vu* was ever seriously offered as a proof of a former psychic existence of the individual; but it is certain that psychologists have taken an interest in it, and have attempted to solve the riddle in a multitude of speculative ways. None of the proposed tentative explanations seems right to me, because none takes account of anything but the accompanying manifestations and the favouring conditions of the phenomenon. Those psychic processes which, according to my observation, are alone responsible for the explanation of the *Déjà vu*—namely, the unconscious fantasies—are generally neglected by the psychologists even to-day.

I believe that it is wrong to designate the feeling of having experienced something before as an illusion. On the contrary, in such moments something is really touched that we have already experienced, only we cannot consciously recall the latter because it never was conscious. In short, the feeling of *Déjà vu* corresponds to the memory of an unconscious fantasy. There are unconscious fantasies (or day dreams) just as there are similar conscious creations, which every one knows from personal experience.

I realize that the object is worthy of most minute study, but I will here give the analysis of only one case of *Déjà vu* in which the feeling was characterized by particular intensity and persistence. A woman of thirty-seven years asserted that she most distinctly remembered that at the age of twelve and a half she paid her first visit to some school friends in the country, and as she entered the garden she immediately had the feeling of having been there before. This feeling was repeated as she went through the living-rooms, so that she believed she knew beforehand how big the next room was, what views one could have on looking out of it, etc. But the belief that this feeling of recognition might have its source in a previous visit to the house and garden, perhaps a visit paid in earliest childhood, was absolutely excluded and disproved by statements from her parents. The woman who related this sought no psychologic explanation, but saw in the appearance of this feeling a prophetic reference to the importance which these friends later assumed in her emotional life. On taking into consideration, however, the circumstance under which this phenomenon presented itself to her, we found the way to another conception.

When she decided upon this visit she knew that these girls had an only brother, who was seriously ill. In the course of the visit she actually saw him. She found him looking very badly, and thought to herself that he would soon die. But it happened that her own only brother had had a serious attack of diphtheria some months before, and during his illness she had lived for weeks with relatives far from her parental home. She believed that her brother was taking part in this visit to the country, imagined even that this was his first long journey since his illness; still, her memory was remarkably indistinct in regard to these points, whereas all other details, and particularly the dress which she wore that day, remained most clearly before her eyes.

To the initiated it will not be difficult to conclude from these suggestions that the expectation of her brother's death had played a great part in the girl's mind at that time, and that either it never became conscious or it was more energetically repressed after the favourable issue of the illness. Under other circumstances she would have been compelled to wear another dress—namely, mourning clothes. She found the analogous situation in her friends' home; their only brother was in danger of an early death, an event that really came to pass a short time after. She might have consciously remembered that she had lived through a similar situation a few months previous, but instead of recalling what was inhibited through repression she transferred the memory feeling to the locality, to the garden, and the house, and merged it into the *fausse reconnaissance* that she had already seen everything exactly as it was.

From the fact of the repression we may conclude that the former expectation of the death of her brother was not far from evincing the character of a wish-fantasy. She would then have become the only child. In her later neurosis she suffered in the most intense manner from the fear of losing her parents, behind which the analysis disclosed, as usual, the unconscious wish of the same content.

My own experience of *Déjà vu* I can trace in a similar manner to the emotional constellation of the moment. It may be expressed as follows: "That would be another occasion for awakening certain fantasies (unconscious and unknown) which were formed in me at one time or another as a wish to improve my situation."[81]

V. Recently when I had occasion to recite to a colleague of a philosophical turn of mind some examples of name-forgetting, with their analyses, he hastened to reply: "That is all very well, but with me the forgetting of a name proceeds in a different manner." Evidently one cannot dismiss this question as simply as that; I do not believe that my colleague had ever thought of an analysis for the forgetting of a name, nor could he say how the process differed in him. But his remark, nevertheless, touches upon a problem which many would be inclined to place in the foreground. Does the solution given for faulty and chance actions apply in general or only in particular cases, and if only in the latter, what are the conditions under which it may also be employed in the explanation of the other phenomena?

In answer to this question my experiences leave me in the lurch. I can only urge against considering the demonstrated connections as rare, for as often as I have made the test in myself and with my patients it was always definitely demonstrated exactly as in the examples reported, or there were at least good reasons to assume this. One should not be surprised, however, when one does not succeed every time in finding the concealed meaning of the symptomatic action, as the amount of inner resistances ranging themselves against the solution must be considered a deciding factor. Also it is not always possible to explain every individual dream of one's self or of patients. To substantiate the general validity of the theory, it is enough if one can penetrate only a certain distance into the hidden associations. The dream which proves refractory when the solution is attempted on the following day can often be robbed of its secret a week or a month later, when the psychic factors combating one another have been reduced as a consequence of a real change that has meanwhile taken place. The same applies to the solution of faulty and symptomatic actions. It would therefore be wrong to affirm of all cases which resist analysis that they are caused by another psychic mechanism than that here revealed; such assumption requires more than negative proofs; moreover, the readiness to believe in a different explanation of faulty and symptomatic actions, which probably exists universally in all normal persons, does not prove anything; it is obviously an expression of the same psychic forces which produced the secret, which therefore strives to protect and struggle against its elucidation.

On the other hand, we must not overlook the fact that the repressed thoughts and feelings are not independent in attaining expression in symptomatic and faulty actions. The technical possibility for such an adjustment of the innervations must be furnished independently of them, and this is then gladly utilized by the intention of the repressed material to come to conscious expression. In the case of linguistic faulty actions an attempt has been made by philosophers and philologists to verify through minute observations what structural and functional relations enter into the service of such intention. If in the determinations of faulty and symptomatic actions we separate the unconscious motive from its co-active physiological and psychophysical relations, the question remains open whether there are still other factors within normal limits which, like the unconscious motive, and in its place can produce faulty and symptomatic actions on the road of the relations. It is not my task to answer this question.

VI. Since the discussion of speech blunders we have been content to demonstrate that faulty actions have a concealed motive, and through the aid of psychoanalysis we have traced our way to the knowledge of their motivation. The general nature and the peculiarities of the psychic factors brought to expression in these faulty actions we have hitherto left almost without consideration; at any rate, we have not attempted to define them more accurately or to examine into their lawfulness. Nor will we now attempt a thorough elucidation of the subject, as the first steps have already taught us that it is more feasible to enter this structure from another side. Here we can put before ourselves certain questions which I will cite in their order. (1) What is the content and the origin of the thoughts and feelings which show themselves through faulty and chance actions? (2) What are the conditions which force a thought or a feeling to make use of these occurrences as a means of expression and place it in a position to do so? (3) Can constant and definite associations be demonstrated between the manner of the faulty action and the qualities brought to expression through it?

I shall begin by bringing together some material for answering the last question. In the discussion of the examples of speech blunders we found it necessary to go beyond the contents of the intended speech, and we had to seek the cause of the speech disturbance outside the intention. The latter was quite clear in a series of cases, and was known to the consciousness of the speaker. In the example that seemed most simple and transparent it was a similar sounding but different conception of the same thought, which disturbed its expression without any one being able to say why the one succumbed and the other came to the surface (Meringer and Mayers' *Contaminations*).

In a second group of cases one conception succumbed to a motive which did not, however, prove strong enough to cause complete submersion. The conception which was withheld was clearly presented to consciousness.

Only of the third group can we affirm unreservedly that the disturbing thought differed from the one intended, and it is obvious that it may establish an essential distinction. The disturbing thought is either connected with the disturbed one through a thought association (disturbance through inner contradiction), or it is substantially strange to it, and just the disturbed word is connected with the disturbing thought through a surprising outer association, which is frequently unconscious.

In the examples which I have given from my psychoanalyses it is found that the entire speech is either under the influence of thoughts which have become active simultaneously, or under absolutely unconscious thoughts which betray themselves either through the disturbance itself, or which evince an indirect influence by making it possible for the individual parts of the unconsciously intended speech to disturb one another. The retained or unconscious thoughts from *which the disturbances in speech emanate are of most varied origin. A general survey does not reveal any definite direction.*

Comparative examinations of examples of mistakes in reading and writing lead to the same conclusions. Isolated cases, as in speech blunders, seem to owe their origin to an unmotivated work of condensation (e.g., the *Apel*). But we should be pleased to know whether special conditions must not be fulfilled in order that such condensation, which is considered regular in the dream-work and faulty in our waking thoughts, should take place. No information concerning this can be obtained from the examples themselves. But I merely refuse from this to draw the conclusion that there are no such conditions, as, for instance, the relaxation of conscious attention; for I have learned elsewhere that automatic actions are especially characterized by correctness and reliability. I would rather emphasize the fact that here, as so frequently in biology, it is the normal relations, or those approaching the normal, that are less favourable objects for investigation than the pathological. What remains obscure in the explanation of these most simple disturbances will, according to my expectation, be made clear through the explanation of more serious disturbances.

Also mistakes in reading and writing do not lack examples in which more remote and more complicated motivation can be recognized.

There is no doubt that the disturbances of the speech functions occur more easily and make less demand on the disturbing forces than other psychic acts.

But one is on different ground when it comes to the examination of forgetting in the literal sense—*i.e.*, the forgetting of past experiences. (To distinguish this forgetting from the others we designate *sensu strictiori* the forgetting of proper names and foreign words, as in Chapters I and II, as "slips"; and the forgetting of resolutions as "omissions.") The principal conditions of the normal process in forgetting are unknown.[82] We are also reminded of the fact that not all is forgotten which we believe to be. Our explanation here deals only with those cases in which the forgetting arouses our astonishment, in so far as it infringes the rule that the unimportant is forgotten, while the important matter is guarded by memory. Analysis of these examples of forgetting which seem to demand a special explanation shows that the motive of forgetting is always an unwillingness to recall something which may evoke painful feelings. We come to the conjecture that this motive universally strives for expression in psychic life, but is inhibited through other and contrary forces from regularly manifesting itself. The extent and significance of this dislike to recall painful impressions seems worthy of the most painstaking psychologic investigation. The question as to what special conditions render possible the universally resistant forgetting in individual cases cannot be solved through this added association.

A different factor steps into the foreground in the forgetting of resolutions; the supposed conflict resulting in the repression of the painful memory becomes tangible, and in the analysis of the examples one regularly recognizes a counter-will which opposes but does not put an end to the resolution. As in previously discussed faulty acts, we here also recognize two types of the psychic process: the counter-will either turns directly against the resolution (in intentions of some consequence) or it is substantially foreign to the resolution itself and establishes its connection with it through an outer association (in almost indifferent resolutions).

The same conflict governs the phenomena of erroneously carried-out actions. The impulse which manifests itself in the disturbances of the action is frequently a counter-impulse. Still oftener it is altogether a strange impulse which only utilizes the opportunity to express itself through a disturbance in the execution of the action. The cases in which the disturbance is the result of an inner contradiction are the most significant ones, and also deal with the more important activities.

The inner conflict in the chance or symptomatic actions then merges into the background. Those motor expressions which are least thought of, or are entirely overlooked by consciousness, serve as the expression of numerous unconscious or restrained feelings. For the most part they represent symbolically wishes and phantoms.

The first question (as to the origin of the thoughts and emotions which find expression in faulty actions) we can answer by saying that in a series of cases the origin of the disturbing thoughts can be readily traced to repressed emotions of the psychic life. Even in healthy persons egotistic, jealous and hostile feelings and impulses, burdened by the pressure of moral education, often utilize the path of faulty actions to express in some way their undeniably existing force which is not recognized by the higher psychic instances. Allowing these faulty and chance actions to continue corresponds in great part to a comfortable toleration of the unmoral. The manifold sexual currents play no insignificant part in these repressed feelings. That they appear so seldom in the thoughts revealed by the analyses of my examples is simply a matter of coincidence. As I have undertaken the analyses of numerous examples from my own psychic life, the selection was partial from the first, and aimed at the exclusion of sexual matters. At other times it seemed that the disturbing thoughts originated from the most harmless objection and consideration.

We have now reached the answer to the second question—that is, what psychologic conditions are responsible for the fact that a thought must seek expression, not in its complete form but, as it were, in parasitic form, as a modification and disturbance of another. From the most striking examples of faulty actions it is quite obvious that this determinant should be sought in a relation to conscious capacity, or in the more or less firmly pronounced character of the "repressed" material. But an examination of this series of examples shows that this character consists of many indistinct elements. The tendency to overlook something because it is wearisome, or because the concerned thought does not really belong to the intended matter—these feelings seem to play the same rôle as motives for the suppression of a thought (which later depends for expression on the disturbance of another), as the moral condemnation of a rebellious emotional feeling, or as the origin of absolutely unconscious trains of thought. An insight into the general nature of the condition of faulty and chance actions cannot be gained in this way.

However, this investigation gives us one single significant fact; the more harmless the motivation of the faulty act the less obnoxious, and hence the less incapable of consciousness, the thought to which it gives expression is; the easier also becomes the solution of the phenomenon after we have turned our attention toward it. The simplest cases of speech blunders are immediately noticed and spontaneously corrected. Where one deals with motivation through actually repressed feelings the solution requires a painstaking analysis, which may sometimes strike against difficulties or turn out unsuccessful.

One is therefore justified in taking the result of this last investigation as an indication of the fact that the satisfactory explanation of the psychologic determinations of faulty and chance actions is to be acquired in another way and from another source. The indulgent reader can therefore see in these discussions the demonstration of the surfaces of fracture in which this theme was quite artificially evolved from a broader connection.

VII. Just a few words to indicate the direction of this broader connection. The mechanism of the faulty and chance actions, as we have learned to know it through the application of analysis, shows in the most essential points an agreement with the mechanism of dream formation, which I have discussed in the chapter "The Dream Work" of my book on the interpretation of dreams. Here, as there, one finds the condensation and compromise formation ("contaminations"); in addition the situation is much the same, since unconscious thoughts find expression as modifications of other thoughts in unusual ways and through outer associations. The incongruities, absurdities, and errors in the dream content by virtue of which the dream is scarcely recognized as a psychic achievement originate in the same way—to be sure, through freer usage of the existing material—as the common error of our everyday life; *here, as there, the appearance of the incorrect function is explained through the peculiar interference of two or more correct actions.*

An important conclusion can be drawn from, this combination: the peculiar mode of operation, whose most striking function we recognize in the dream content, should not be adjudged only to the sleeping state of the psychic life when we possess abundant proof of its activity during the waking state in the form of faulty actions. The same connection also forbids us assuming that these psychic processes which impress us as abnormal and strange are determined by deep-seated decay of psychic activity or by morbid state of function.[83]

The correct understanding of this strange psychic work which allows the faulty actions to originate like the dream pictures will only be possible after we have discovered that the psychoneurotic symptoms, particularly the psychic formations of hysteria and compulsion neurosis, repeat in their mechanisms all the essential features of this mode of operation. The continuation of our investigation would therefore have to begin at this point.

There is still another special interest for us in considering the faulty, chance, and symptomatic actions in the light of this last analogy. If we compare them to the function of the psychoneuroses and the neurotic symptoms, two frequently recurring statements gain in sense and support—namely, that the border-line between the nervous, normal, and abnormal states is indistinct, and that we are all slightly nervous. Regardless of all medical experience, one may construe various types of such barely suggested nervousness, the *formes frustes* of the neuroses. There may be cases in which only a few symptoms appear, or they may manifest themselves rarely or in mild forms; the extenuation may be transferred to the number, intensity, or to the temporal outbreak of the morbid manifestation. It may also happen that just this type, which forms the most frequent transition between health and disease, may never be discovered. The transition type, whose morbid manifestations come in the form of faulty and symptomatic actions, is characterized by the fact that the symptoms are transformed to the least important psychic activities, while everything that can lay claim to a higher psychic value remains free from disturbance. When the symptoms are disposed of in a reverse manner—that is, when they appear in the most important individual and social activities in a manner to disturb the functions of nourishment and sexual relations, professional and social life—such disposition is found in the severe cases of neuroses, and is perhaps more characteristic of the latter than the multiformity or vividness of the morbid manifestations.

But the common character of the mildest as well as the severest cases, to which the faulty and chance actions contribute, lies in the ability to refer the phenomena to unwelcome, repressed, psychic material, which, though pushed away from consciousness, is nevertheless not robbed of all capacity to express itself.

NOTES:

1. *Monatsschrift f. Psychiatrie.*
2. This is the usual way of bringing to consciousness hidden ideas. Cf. *The Interpretation of Dreams*, pp. 83-4, translated by A. A. Brill, The Macmillan Company, New York, and Allen, London.
3. Finer observation reduces somewhat the contrast between the analyses of *Signorelli* and *aliquis* as far as the substitutive recollections are concerned. Here, too, the forgetting seems to be accompanied by substitutive formations. When I later asked my companion whether in his effort to recall the forgotten word he did not think of some substitution, he informed me that he was at first tempted to put an ab into the verse: *nostris ab ossibus* (perhaps the disjointed part of *a-liquis*) and that later the word *exoriare* obtruded itself with particular distinctness and persistency. Being sceptical, he added that it was apparently due to the fact that it was the first word of the verse. But when I asked him to focus his attention on the associations to *exoriare* he gave me the word *exorcism*. This makes me think that the reinforcement of *exoriare* in the reproduction has really the value of such substitution. It probably came through the association *exorcism* from the names of the saints. However, those are refinements upon which no value need be laid. It seems now quite possible that the appearance of any kind of substitutive recollection is a constant sign—perhaps only characteristic and misleading—of the purposive forgetting motivated by repression. This substitution might also exist in the reinforcement of an element akin to the thing forgotten, even

where incorrect substitutive names fail to appear. Thus, in the example Signorelli, as long as the name of the painter remained inaccessible to me, I had more than a clear visual memory of the cycle of his frescoes, and of the picture of himself in the corner; at least it was more intensive than any of my other visual memory traces. In another case, also reported in my essay of 1898, I had hopelessly forgotten the street name and address connected with a disagreeable visit in a strange city, but—as if to mock me—the house number appeared especially vivid, whereas the memory of numbers usually causes me the greatest difficulty.

4. I am not fully convinced of the lack of an inner connection between the two streams of thought in the case of *Signorelli.* In carefully following the repressed thought concerning the theme of death and sexual life, one does strike an idea which shows a near relation to the theme of the frescoes of *Orvieto.*
5. *The Psychology of Dementia Præcox*, translated by F. Peterson and A. A. Brill.
6. *The Psychology of Dementia Præcox, p. 45.*
7. *Zentralb. f. Psychoanalyse, I. 9, 1911.*
8. "Analyse eines Falles von Namenvergessen," *Zentralb. f. Psychoanalyse*, Jahrg. 11, Heft 2, 1911.
9. *Published in the Monatsschrift f. Psychiatrie u. Neurologie, 1899.*
10. "Enquête sur les premiers souvenirs de l'enfance," *L'Année psychologique*, iii., 1897.
11. "Study of Early Memories," *Psychological Review*, 1901.
12. I assert this as a result of certain investigations made by myself.
13. The examples are given by the editor.
14. Those who are interested are referred to pp. 62, 73, and 97 of the author's work.
15. *Neue Freie Presse*, August 23, 1900: "Wie man sich versprechen kann."

16. *Völker psychologie*, vol. i., pt. i., p. 371, etc., 1900.

17. Italics are mine.

18. It turned out that she was under the influence of unconscious thoughts concerning pregnancy and prevention of conception. With the words "shut up like a pocket knife," which she uttered consciously as a complaint, she meant to describe the position of the child in the womb. The word "earnest" in my remark recalled to her the name (S. Ernst) of the well-known Vienna business firm in Kärthner Strasse, which used to advertise the sale of articles for the prevention of conception.

19. Similar mistakes dealing with *Officer 666* were recently reported to me by other psycho-analysts.

20. It may be observed that aristocrats in particular very frequently distort the names of the physicians they consult, from which we may conclude that inwardly they slight them, in spite of the politeness with which they are wont to greet them. I shall cite here some excellent observations concerning the forgetting of names from the works of Professor E. Jones, of Toronto: *Papers on Psycho-analysis*, chap. iii. p. 49:—

    "Few people can avoid feeling a twinge of resentment when they find that their name has been forgotten, particularly if it is by some one with whom they had hoped or expected it would be remembered. They instinctively realize that if they had made a greater impression on the person's mind he would certainly have remembered them again, for the name is an integral part of the personality. Similarly, few things are more flattering to most people than to find themselves addressed by name by a great personage where they could hardly have anticipated it. Napoleon, like most leaders of men, was a master of this art. In the midst of the disastrous campaign of France in 1814, he gave an amazing proof of his memory in this direction. When in a town near Craonne, he recollected that he had met the mayor, De Bussy, over twenty years ago in the La Fère Regiment. The delighted De Bussy at once threw himself into his service with extraordinary zeal. Conversely, there is no surer way of affronting some one than by pretending to forget his name; the insinuation is thus conveyed that the person is so unimportant in our eyes that we cannot be bothered to remember his name. This device is often exploited in literature. In Turgentev's *Smoke* (p. 255) the following passage occurs: "'So you still find Baden entertaining, M'sieur—Litvinov.' Ratmirov always uttered Litvinov's surname with hesitation, every time, as though he had forgotten it, and could not at once recall it. In this way, as well as by the lofty flourish of his hat in saluting him, he meant to insult his pride." The same author, in his *Fathers and Children* (p. 107), writes: "The Governor invited Kirsanov and Bazarov to his ball, and within a few minutes invited them a second time, regarding them as brothers, and calling them Kisarov." Here the forgetting that he had spoken to them, the mistake in the names, and the inability to distinguish between the two young men, constitute a culmination of disparagement. Falsification of a name has the same signification as forgetting it; it is only a step towards complete amnesia."

21. *Zentralb. f. Psychoanalyse*, ii., Jahrg. I. Cf. also Brill's *Psychanalysis: Its Theories and Practical Application*, p. 202. Saunders, Philadelphia and London.

22. *Jones, Papers on Psycho-analysis, p. 60.*

23.

> "Ce qu'on conçoit bien
> S'énonce clairement,
> Et les mots pour le dire
> Arrivent aisément."
> *Boileau, Art Poétique.*

24. *The Interpretation of Dreams, p. 208.*

25. Bleuler, *Affektivität Suggestibilität, Paranoia*, p. 121, Halle. Marhold, 1906.

26. A similar situation occurs in *Julius Cæsar*, iii. 3:

"CINNA. Truly, my name is Cinna.

"BURGHER. Tear him to pieces! he is a conspirator.

"CINNA. I am Cinna the poet! not Cinna the conspirator.

"BURGHER. No matter; his name is Cinna; tear the name out of his heart and let him go."

27. Ethyl alcohol is, of course, the chemical name for ordinary alcohol.

28. Jones, *Psycho-analysis*, p. 66.

29. *Zentralbl. f. Psychoanalyse, i. 12.*

30. In the course of the conference the details of the previous first visit return to consciousness.

31. Brill, *loc. cit.*, p. 197.

32. If we inquire of a person whether he suffered from luetic infection ten or fifteen years ago, we are only too apt to forget that psychically the patient has looked upon this disease in an entirely different manner than on, let us say, an acute attack of rheumatism. In the anamneses which parents give about their neurotic daughters, it is hardly possible to distinguish with any degree of certainty the portion forgotten from that hidden, for anything that stands in the way of the girl's future marriage is systematically set aside by the parents, that is, it becomes repressed. A man who had recently lost his beloved wife from an affection of the lungs reported to me the following case of misleading the doctor, which can only be explained by the theory of such forgetting. "As my poor wife's pleuritis had not disappeared after many weeks, Dr. P. was called in consultation. While taking the history he asked among others the customary questions whether there were any cases of lung trouble in my wife's family. My wife denied any such cases, and even I myself could not remember any. While Dr. P. was taking leave the conversation accidentally turned to excursions, and my wife said: 'Yes, even to Landgersdorf, where my poor brother lies buried, is a long journey.' This brother died about fifteen years

ago, after having suffered for years from tuberculosis. My wife was very fond of him, and often spoke about him. Indeed, I recall that when her malady was diagnosed as pleurisy she was very worried and sadly remarked: 'My brother also died of lung trouble.' But the memory was so very repressed that even after the above-cited conversation about the trip to L. she found no occasion to correct her information concerning the diseases in her family. I myself was struck by this forgetting at the very moment she began to talk about Landgersdorf." A perfectly analogous experience is related by Ernest Jones in his work. A physician whose wife suffered from some obscure abdominal malady remarked to her: "It is comforting to think that there has been no tuberculosis in your family." She turned to him very astonished and said, "Have you forgotten that my mother died of tuberculosis, and that my sister recovered from it only after having been given up by the doctors?"

33. During the days when I was first writing these pages the following almost incredible case of forgetting happened to me. On the 1st of January I examined my notes so that I could send out my bills. In the month of June I came across the name M——l, and could not recall the person to whom it belonged. My surprise increased when I observed from my books that I treated the case in a sanatorium, and that for weeks I had called on the patient daily. A patient treated under such conditions is rarely forgotten by a physician in six months. I asked myself if it could have been a man—a paretic—a case without interest? Finally, the note about the fee received brought to my memory all the knowledge which strove to elude it. M——l was a fourteen-year-old girl, the most remarkable case of my latter years, a case which taught me a lesson I am not likely ever to forget, a case whose upshot gave me many painful hours. The child became afflicted with an unmistakable hysteria, which quickly and thoroughly improved under my care. After this improvement the child was taken away from me by the parents. She still complained of abdominal pains which had played the part in the hysterical symptoms. Two months later she died of sarcoma

of the abdominal glands. The hysteria, to which she was greatly predisposed, took the tumour-formation as a provocative agent, and I, fascinated by the tumultuous but harmless manifestations of hysteria, perhaps overlooked the first sign of the insidious and incurable disease.

34. A. Pick ("Zur Psychologie des Vergessens bei Geistes- und Nervenkranken," *Archiv. f. Kriminal-Anthropologie u. Kriminalistik*, von H. Gross) has recently collected a number of authors who realize the value of the influence of the affective factors on memory, and who more or less clearly recognize that a defensive striving against pain can lead to forgetting. But none of us has been able to represent this phenomenon and its psychologic determination as exhaustively, and at the same time as effectively, as Nietzsche in one of his aphorisms (*Jenseits von Gut und Böse*, ii., *Hauptstück* 68): "'I have done that,' says my Memory. 'I could not have done that,' says my Pride, and remains inexorable. Finally, my Memory yields."

35. Cf. Hans Gross, *Kriminal Psychologie*, 1898.

36. Darwin on forgetting. In Darwin's autobiography one finds the following passage that does equal credit to his scientific honesty and his psychologic acumen: "I had during many years followed a golden rule, namely, that whenever a published fact, a new observation or thought, came across me which was opposed to my general results, to make a memorandum of it without fail and at once; for I had found by experience that such facts and thoughts were far more apt to escape from the memory than favourable ones" (quoted by Jones, *loc. cit.*, p. 38).

37. *Cf. Bernheim, Neue Studien über Hypnotismus, Suggestion und Psychotherapie, 1892.*

38. Young men of education who can pass the examination and pay for their maintenance serve one instead of two years' compulsory service.

39. In Bernard Shaw's *Cæsar and Cleopatra*, Cæsar's indifference to Cleopatra is depicted by his being vexed on leaving Egypt at

having forgotten to do something. He finally recollected what he had forgotten—to take leave of Cleopatra—this, to be sure, is in full accord with historical truth. How little Cæsar thought of the little Egyptian princess! Cited from Jones, *loc. cit.*, p. 50.

40. Women, with their fine understanding of unconscious mental processes, are, as a rule, more apt to take offence when we do not recognize them in the street, and hence do not greet them, than to accept the most obvious explanation, namely, that the dilatory one is short-sighted or so engrossed in thought that he did not see them. They conclude that they surely would have been noticed if they had been considered of any consequence.

41. Dr. Ferenczi reports that he was a distracted person himself, and was considered peculiar by his friends on account of the frequency and strangeness of his failing. But the signs of this inattention have almost all disappeared since he began to practise psychoanalysis with patients, and was forced to turn his attention to the analysis of his own ego. He believes that one renounces these failings when one learns to extend by so much one's own responsibilities. He therefore justly maintains that distractedness is a state which depends on unconscious complexes, and is curable by psychoanalysis. One day he was reproaching himself for having committed a technical error in the psychoanalysis of a patient, and on this day all his former distractions reappeared. He stumbled while walking in the street (a representation of that *faux pas* in the treatment), he forgot his pocket-book at home, he was a penny short in his car fare, he did not properly button his clothes, etc.

42. E. Jones remarks regarding this: "Often the resistance is of a general order. Thus a busy man forgets to mail a letter entrusted to him—to his slight annoyance—by his wife, just as he may 'forget' to carry out her shopping orders."

43. For the sake of the unity of the theme I may here digress from the accepted classification, and add that the human memory evinces a particular partiality in regard to money matters. False reminiscences

of having already paid something are often very obstinate, as I know from personal experience. When free sway is given to avaricious intent outside of the serious interests of life, when it is indulged in in the spirit of fun, as in card playing, we then find that the most honourable men show an inclination to errors, mistakes in memory and accounts, and without realizing how, they even find themselves involved in small frauds. Such liberties depend in no small part also on the psychically refreshing character of the play. The saying that in play we can learn a person's character may be admitted if we can add "the repressed character." If waiters ever make unintentional mistakes they are apparently due to the same mechanism. Among merchants we can frequently observe a certain delay in the paying out of sums of money, in payments of bills and the like, which brings the owner no profit and can be only understood psychologically as the expression of a counter-will against giving out money. Brill sums it up with epigrammatic keenness: "We are more apt to mislay letters containing bills than cheques" (Brill, *Psychanalysis, its Theories and Practical Application*, p. 197).

44. Translated by A. A. Brill.

45. A second publication of Meringer has later shown me how very unjust I was to this author when I attributed to him so much understanding.

46. Jones, *loc. cit.*, p. 79.

47. Alas! the Venus of Medici is lost!

48. The Œdipus dream as I was wont to call it, because it contains the key to the understanding of the legend of King Œdipus. In the text of Sophocles the relation of such a dream is put in the mouth of Jocasta (cf. *The Interpretation of Dreams*, pp. 222-4, etc.).

49. *New York Medical Journal*, September, 1912. Reprinted in large form as Chapter X of *Psychanalysis*, etc., Saunders, Philadelphia.

50. The self-inflicted injury which does not entirely tend toward self-annihilation has, moreover, no other choice in our present state of civilization than to hide itself behind the accidental, or to break

through in a simulation of spontaneous illness. Formerly, it was a customary sign of mourning, at other times it expressed itself in ideas of piety and renunciation of the world.

51. The case is then identical with a sexual attack on a woman, in whom the attack of the man cannot be warded off through the full muscular strength of the woman because a portion of the unconscious feelings of the one attacked meets it with ready acceptance. To be sure, it is said that such a situation paralyses the strength of a woman; we need only add the reasons for this paralysis. Insofar the clever sentence of Sancho Panza, which he pronounced as governor of his island, is psychologically unjust (*Don Quixote*, vol. ii. chap. xlv). A woman hauled before the judge a man who was supposed to have robbed her of her honour by force of violence. Sancho indemnified her with a full purse which he took from the accused, but after the departure of the woman he gave the accused permission to follow her and snatch the purse from her. Both returned wrestling, the woman priding herself that the villain was unable to possess himself of the purse. Thereupon Sancho spoke: "Had you shown yourself so stout and valiant to defend your body (nay, but half so much) as you have done to defend your purse, the strength of Hercules could not have forced you."

52. It is evident that the situation of a battlefield is such as to meet the requirement of conscious suicidal intent which, nevertheless, shuns the direct way. Cf. in *Wallenstein* the words of the Swedish captain concerning the death of Max Piccolomini: "They say he wished to die."

53. "Selbstbestrafung wegen Abortus von Dr. J. E. G. van Emden," Haag (Holland), *Zentralb. f. Psychoanalyse*, ii. 12.

54. "Beitrag zur Symbolik im Alltag von Ernest Jones," *Zentralb. f. Psychoanalyse*, i. 3, 1911.

55. Psychoanalytic research, with the penetration of infantile amnesia, has shown that this apparent precocity is a less abnormal occurrence than was previously supposed.

56. The term "medical questions" is a common periphrasis for "sexual questions."

57. Cf. Oldham's "I wear my pen as others do their sword."

58. Maeder, "Contribution à la psychologie de la vie quotidienne," *Arch. des psychologie*, T. vi. 1906.

59. Here is another small collection of various symptomatic actions in normal and neurotic persons. An elderly colleague who does not like to lose at cards had to pay one evening a large sum of money in consequence of his losses; he did this without complaint, but with a peculiar constrained temper. After his departure it was discovered that he had left at this place practically everything he had with him, spectacles, cigar-case, and handkerchief. That would be readily translated into the words: "You robbers, you have nicely plundered me." A man who suffers from occasional sexual impotence, which has its origin in the intimacy of his infantile relations to his mother, relates that he is in the habit of embellishing pamphlets and notes with an S, the initial of his mother's name. He cannot bear the idea of having letters from home come in contact with other unsanctified correspondence, and therefore finds it necessary to keep the former separate. A young woman suddenly flings open the door of the consulting-room while her predecessor is still present. She excused herself on the ground of "thoughtlessness"; it soon came to light that she demonstrated her curiosity which caused her at an earlier time to intrude into the bedroom of her parents. Girls who are proud of their beautiful hair know so well how to manipulate combs and hairpins, that in the midst of conversation their hair becomes loosened. During the treatment (in a reclining position) some men scatter change from their pockets and thus pay for the hour of treatment; the amount scattered is in proportion to their estimation of the work. Whoever forgets articles in the doctor's office, such as eyeglasses, gloves, handbags, generally indicates that he cannot tear himself away and is anxious to return soon. Ernest Jones says: "One can almost measure the success with which a physician is practising psychotherapy, for instance, by the size of the collection

of umbrellas, handkerchiefs, purses, and so on, that he could make in a month. The slightest habits and acts performed with a minimum of attention, such as the winding of a clock before retiring to sleep, the putting out of lights before leaving the room, and similar actions, are occasionally subject to disturbances which clearly demonstrate the influence of the unconscious complex, and what is thought to be the strongest 'habits.'"

In the journal *Cœnobium*, Maeder relates about a hospital physician who, on account of an important matter, desired to get to the city that evening, although he was on duty and had no right to leave the hospital. On his return he noticed to his surprise that there was a light in his room. On leaving the room he had forgotten to put it out, something that had never happened before. But he soon grasped the motive of this forgetting. The hospital superintendent who lived in the same house must have concluded from the light in the room that he was at home. A man overburdened with worries and subject to occasional depressions assured me that he regularly forgot to wind his watch on those evenings when life seemed too hard and unfriendly. In this omission to wind his watch he symbolically expressed that it was a matter of indifference to him whether he lived to see the next day. Another man who was personally unknown to me wrote: "Having been struck by a terrible misfortune, life appeared so harsh and unsympathetic, that I imagined that I had not sufficient strength to live to see the next day. I then noticed that almost every day I forgot to wind my watch, something that I never omitted before. I had been in the habit of doing it regularly before retiring in an almost mechanical and unconscious manner. It was only very seldom that I thought of it, and that happened when I had something important for the next day which held my interest. 'Should this be considered a symptomatic action? I really cannot explain it.'" Whoever will take the trouble, like Jung (*The Psychology of Dementia Præcox*, translated by Peterson and Brill), or Maeder ("Une voie nouvelle en Psychologie—Freud et son ecole," *Cœnobium*, Lugano, 1906), to pay attention to melodies which one hums to himself aimlessly and unconsciously, will regularly discover the relation of the melody's text to a theme which occupies the person at that time.

60. "*Das Verlieren als* Symptom-handlung," Zentralb. f. Psychoanalyse, i. 10-11.

61. Translated by A. A. Brill. The Macmillan Company, New York; George Allen Company, London.

62. This is not a perfect error. According to the orphic version of the myth the emasculation was per*formed by* Zeus on his father Kronos.

63. Loc. cit., p. *191.*

64. *N*ouvelles contributi*ons, etc.*, Arch. d*e Psych., vi. 1908.*

65. *Loc. cit., p. 42.*

66. *Zentralb. f. Psychoanalyse, ii. 9.*

67. *Zentralb. f. Psychoanalyse, ii. 5.*

68. This continued action in the unconscious manifested itself once in the form of a dream which followed the faulty action, another time in the repetition of the same or in the omission of a correction.

69. Alfred Adler, "Drei Psychoanalysen von Zahlen einfällen und obsedierenden Zahlen," *Psych. Neur. Wochenschr.*, No. 28, 1905.

70. As an explanation of *Macbeth*, No. 17 of the U. L., I was informed by Dr. Adler that in his seventeenth year this man had joined an anarchistic society whose aim was regicide. Probably this is why he forgot the content of the play *Macbeth*. The same person invented at that time a secret code in which numbers substituted letters.

71. For the sake of simplicity I have omitted some of the not less suitable thoughts of the patients.

72. *Loc. cit.*, p. 36.

73. "Ein Beitrag zur Kenntnis des Zahlentraumes," *Zentralb. f. Psychoanalyse*, i. 12.

74. "Unconscious Manipulation of Numbers" (*ibid.*, ii. 5, 1912).

75. This is another excellent example showing how a conscious intention was powerless to counteract an unconscious resistance.

76. These conceptions of strict determinism in seemingly arbitrary actions have already borne rich fruit for psychology—perhaps also for the administration of justice. Bleuler and Jung have in this way made intelligible the reaction in the so-called association experiments, wherein the test person answers to a given word with one occurring to him (stimulus-word reaction), while the time elapsing between the stimulus word and answer is measured (reaction-time). Jung has shown in his *Diagnostische Assoziationsstudien*, 1906, what fine reagents for psychic occurrences we possess in this association-experiment. Three students of criminology, H. Gross, of Prague, and Wertheimer and Klein, have developed from these experiments a technique for the diagnosis of facts (*Tatbestands-Diagnostik*) in criminal cases, the examination of which is now tested by psychologists and jurists.

77. Proceeding from other points of view, this interpretation of the trivial and accidental by the patient has been designated as "delusions of reference."

78. For example, the fantasies of the hysterical regarding sexual and cruel abuse which are made conscious by analysis often correspond in every detail with the complaints of persecuted paranoiacs. It is remarkable but not altogether unexpected that we also meet the identical content as reality in the contrivances of perverts for the gratification of their desires.

79. Which naturally has nothing of the character of perception.

80. Zentralb. f. Psychoanalyse, ii. 5.

81. Thus far this explanation of *Déjà vu* has been appreciated by only one observer. Dr. Ferenczi, to whom the third edition of this book is indebted for so many contributions, writes to me concerning this: "I have been convinced, through myself as well as others, that the inexplicable feeling of familiarity can be referred to unconscious fantasies of which we are unconsciously reminded

in an actual situation. With one of my patients the process was apparently different, but in reality it was quite analogous. This feeling returned to him very often, but showed itself regularly as originating in a forgotten (repressed) portion of a dream of the preceding night. Thus it appears that the *Déjà vu* can originate not only from day dreams but also from night dreams."

82. I can perhaps give the following outline concerning the mechanism of actual forgetting. The memory material succumbs in general to two influences, condensation and disfigurement. Disfigurement is the work of the tendencies dominating the psychic life, and directs itself above all against the affective remnants of memory traces which maintain a more resistive attitude towards condensation. The traces which have grown indifferent merge into a process of condensation without opposition; in addition it may be observed that tendencies of disfigurement also feed on the indifferent material, because they have not been gratified where they wished to manifest themselves. As these processes of condensation and disfigurement continue for long periods during which all fresh experiences act upon the transformation of the memory content, it is our belief that it is time that makes memory uncertain and indistinct. It is quite probable that in forgetting there can really be no question of a direct function of time. From the repressed memory traces it can be verified that they suffer no changes even in the longest periods. The unconscious, at all events, knows no time limit. The most important as well as the most peculiar character of psychic fixation consists in the fact that all impressions are on the one hand retained in the same form as they were received, and also in the forms that they have assumed in their further development. This state of affairs cannot be elucidated by any comparison from any other sphere. By virtue of this theory every former state of the memory content may thus be restored, even though all original relations have long been replaced by newer ones.

83. Cf. here *The Interpretation of Dreams*, p. 483. Macmillan: New York; and Allen: London.